Python, C#, and the Future of Programming

Integrating Modern Development Tools to Build Next-Generation Cross-Platform Applications

THOMPSON CARTER

Table of Contents

INTRODUCTION

Mastering Cross-Platform Development with Python and C#: Techniques, Frameworks, and Best Practices"

In today's fast-paced world of software development, the demand for applications that work seamlessly across multiple platforms is greater than ever. From mobile devices and desktops to cloud infrastructure, users expect software that performs flawlessly on a variety of devices and operating systems. As a developer, mastering **cross-platform development** is no longer just a trend; it's a necessity. This book, *"Mastering Cross-Platform Development with Python and C#: Techniques, Frameworks, and Best Practices"*, is your comprehensive guide to building powerful, scalable, and flexible applications that work across multiple platforms using two of the most popular programming languages: **Python** and **C#**.

Why Cross-Platform Development?

The traditional model of developing separate applications for iOS, Android, Windows, and Linux not only leads to increased development time but also introduces the complexity of maintaining multiple codebases. Cross-platform development addresses this challenge by allowing developers to write code once and deploy it across a wide range of platforms. Whether you're building a **web application**, **mobile app**, or **cloud-based solution**, being proficient in cross-platform frameworks allows you to reach a broader audience with less effort.

Python and **C#** are two of the most versatile programming languages used for cross-platform development. **Python** is well known for its simplicity and wide array of libraries, making it an excellent choice for **backend development**, **machine learning**, and **data science**, while **C#** is widely used in the **Microsoft ecosystem** and for **game development** with **Unity**, as well as **enterprise applications** through the **.NET Core** framework.

The Focus of This Book

This book is designed to help developers like you build applications that can run on a wide array of devices and platforms, with a specific focus on the powerful combination of **Python** and **C#**. We will explore the latest tools, frameworks, and best practices for building cross-platform applications across mobile, desktop, web, and cloud environments. With practical, hands-on examples, you will learn how to leverage both languages to solve real-world problems efficiently and effectively.

Throughout this book, we will cover topics such as:

- **Core Concepts of Cross-Platform Development**: Understanding the fundamentals of building software that works across multiple platforms and devices.
- **Building Web Applications with Python and C#**: Learn to create modern, scalable web applications using **Flask**, **Django**, **ASP.NET Core**, and **Blazor**.
- **Mobile Development**: Dive into **Xamarin** and **.NET MAUI** for building cross-platform mobile apps, and explore how **Flutter** and **React Native** can be utilized alongside **Python**.
- **Cloud-Native Applications**: Harness the power of **cloud platforms** like **AWS**, **Azure**, and **Google Cloud** to build serverless, scalable applications with Python and C#.
- **Integrating AI and Machine Learning**: Learn how to integrate **machine learning** models into cross-platform applications, using **TensorFlow** and **scikit-learn** for Python, and **ML.NET** for C#.

- **Best Practices for Performance, Security, and Scalability**: Dive deep into the design principles that ensure your applications are optimized for speed, reliability, and security, regardless of platform.
- **Real-World Projects and Case Studies**: Throughout the book, we'll showcase projects like a **task management system**, a **smart home automation system**, and a **SaaS application**, to give you practical, hands-on experience with cross-platform development.

Target Audience

This book is designed for **developers of all levels** who want to expand their skill set and tackle the challenges of building cross-platform applications. Whether you're a beginner just starting your journey in **Python** and C#, or an experienced developer looking to deepen your knowledge of **cross-platform frameworks**, this book will equip you with the tools and techniques needed to succeed in today's multi-platform world.

What You Will Learn

By the end of this book, you will:

- **Master cross-platform development**: Learn to use Python and C# to create applications that work on desktop, mobile, web, and cloud.
- **Build production-ready applications**: Leverage the most powerful frameworks and libraries to build scalable, secure, and high-performance applications.
- **Gain practical experience**: Work through real-world case studies and hands-on projects, gaining the experience necessary to build your own cross-platform apps.
- **Future-proof your career**: With the rise of mobile devices, cloud computing, and AI, the demand for cross-platform developers is growing rapidly. This book will ensure you stay ahead of the curve and equip you with the skills to succeed in the next generation of software development.

Why Python and C#?

- **Python**: Known for its ease of use, versatility, and powerful libraries, Python is widely used in web development, automation, data science, machine learning, and cloud computing. Python's **Flask**, **Django**, and **FastAPI** are perfect for building robust backends, while libraries like **Kivy** and **PyQt** allow for desktop development. With its integration in

16

cloud platforms and machine learning, Python has become a cornerstone of modern software development.

- **C#**: As a **statistically-typed language**, C# has long been favored for its ability to build **enterprise applications** and **games** (via **Unity**). With the advent of **.NET Core** and **.NET MAUI**, C# has evolved into a cross-platform powerhouse. Developers can now build **mobile apps** (using **Xamarin**), **web apps** (using **ASP.NET Core**), and even **cloud services** on a single platform, thanks to the power of C#'s interoperability and performance.

Why This Book?

This book is a one-stop guide to mastering cross-platform development with Python and C#. By combining in-depth technical knowledge, practical hands-on exercises, and real-world projects, it will help you develop the skills you need to succeed as a cross-platform developer. Whether you want to build the next big mobile app, SaaS solution, or cloud-based service, the tools and techniques covered here will provide a solid foundation for your journey.

So, whether you're looking to **build enterprise-grade solutions**, **create mobile apps**, or **integrate AI into your cross-platform projects**, this book will guide you every step of the way.

Let's embark on this exciting journey of mastering **Python, C#**, and **cross-platform development** together.

Part 1: Foundations of Python, C#, and Modern Development

Chapter 1

The Evolution of Programming: Python, C#, and the Cross-Platform Era

1.1 The Rise of Multi-Platform Development

The demand for **cross-platform applications** has never been higher. In today's fast-paced world, users expect applications that seamlessly run across multiple platforms, whether it's **Windows, macOS, Linux, Android, or iOS**. This trend has driven the development of technologies and frameworks that allow developers to write **one codebase** and deploy it across a range of platforms.

Traditional Development	Cross-Platform Development
Development for specific platforms (e.g., only Windows or only iOS).	Build applications once and run them across multiple platforms

Traditional Development	Cross-Platform Development
	without rewriting code for each one.
Often results in higher development costs and longer timelines.	Significantly reduces costs, time-to-market, and ensures wider reach.
Platform-specific features often require complex integration.	Use of frameworks like **Flutter, Xamarin, MAUI, and Electron** for easier integration.

The rise of **cloud services** and the availability of **containerization** technologies (like **Docker** and **Kubernetes**) have enabled developers to not only deploy their applications across different environments but also **scale** them effortlessly across multiple devices.

1.2 Why Python and C# Are Leading Modern Application Development

Python

Python has evolved from a **scripting language** to a **full-fledged, multi-purpose development tool**. Its success can be attributed to:

- **Simplicity and Readability**: Python's syntax is clean and intuitive, making it an excellent choice for both beginners and experienced developers. It's a language that is **easy to learn** but also **powerful enough** to handle complex tasks.

- **Wide Ecosystem**: Python boasts a **massive ecosystem** of libraries and frameworks, including **Django** for web development, **TensorFlow** and **PyTorch** for machine learning, and **Flask** for lightweight applications. This versatility makes Python suitable for everything from web apps to scientific computing.

- **Cross-Platform Support**: With Python, you can run applications across platforms with minimal modification. It works well on **Windows, macOS, and Linux**, and its community has made it easier to deploy Python applications in containers (e.g., Docker) and the cloud.

- **Ideal for Prototyping**: Python's quick setup and ease of use make it perfect for **rapid prototyping**, enabling developers to quickly turn ideas into working models and proof of concepts.

C#

C# is the backbone of the **Microsoft ecosystem**, and it has expanded beyond just Windows development. Key reasons for its dominance include:

- **Versatility**: With the introduction of **.NET Core** (now part of **.NET 5 and beyond**), C# became **cross-platform**, allowing developers to build applications for Windows, macOS, and Linux. It is used for everything from **web and desktop applications** to **mobile and cloud development**.
- **Enterprise Adoption**: C# is often used for **enterprise-level applications**, largely due to its **robust features**, such as **strong typing, object-oriented design**, and integration with Microsoft services like **Azure**. It has also evolved with **modern programming paradigms** like **async/await** for asynchronous programming.

- **Blazor**: With the arrival of **Blazor**, C# can now be used to build **interactive web applications** that run directly in the browser using **WebAssembly**, making C# a front-end language as well.

- **Tooling and Integration**: C# benefits from **excellent tooling** provided by **Visual Studio**, which offers a suite of features for debugging, profiling, and refactoring code. Additionally, C# integrates seamlessly with **Azure** for cloud-based applications and services.

1.3 Use Cases for Python vs. C# in Today's Industry

While both Python and C# can be used in many areas, each language shines in certain use cases. Below are the strengths of each language in different scenarios:

Python Use Cases

1. **Data Science and Machine Learning**: Python has become the **de facto language** for data science, thanks to powerful libraries like **NumPy**, **Pandas**, **Matplotlib**, **TensorFlow**, and **Scikit-learn**. Its simplicity allows developers to focus on **data**

24

analysis, **visualization**, and **AI modeling**, making it highly favored by data scientists and machine learning engineers.

2. **Web Development**: With frameworks like **Django** and **Flask**, Python makes web development **quick and efficient**. **Django** provides a full-stack solution, while **Flask** is lightweight and ideal for smaller applications.

3. **Automation and Scripting**: Python is an excellent choice for writing **scripts** to automate repetitive tasks, manage data, or even control hardware systems. It's heavily used in **DevOps, network automation**, and **web scraping**.

4. **Scientific Computing**: Due to its ease of integration with **scientific libraries**, Python is extensively used in academic and research institutions for fields like **physics, engineering**, and **bioinformatics**.

C# Use Cases

1. **Enterprise Applications**: C# has long been a staple for **enterprise-level applications**, especially those built within the **Microsoft ecosystem**. Its **robust framework** (e.g., **ASP.NET Core**) provides developers with a powerful toolkit for building

scalable, secure, and high-performance applications.

2. **Cloud-Based Applications**: With **.NET Core** and **Azure**, C# has become a **go-to language** for building cloud-based services. Developers can easily build web services, APIs, and microservices hosted on **Azure** or other cloud platforms.

3. **Cross-Platform Mobile Development**: Using **Xamarin** or **.NET MAUI**, C# developers can write **cross-platform mobile apps** for iOS, Android, and Windows. This saves time and effort in building separate apps for different mobile platforms.

4. **Game Development**: **Unity**, the most popular game engine, uses **C# as its primary language**. It enables developers to create games for mobile, console, and PC, making C# one of the dominant languages in the game development space.

5. **Web Development**: **ASP.NET Core** is a **high-performance, cross-platform framework** for building dynamic, scalable web applications. C# is often chosen for developing **enterprise-grade web applications**.

Conclusion: Choosing Python or C# for Your Next Project

Both **Python and C#** offer tremendous power for developers, but choosing the right tool depends on the **specific use case**. Python shines in **data science**, **machine learning**, and **rapid development**, while C# is an ideal choice for **enterprise applications**, **cloud computing**, and **cross-platform mobile apps**.

In this book, you'll see how **Python and C# complement each other** in modern development practices. Whether you are building a **data pipeline**, a **cloud-native application**, or an **interactive mobile app**, understanding both languages will provide you with the **flexibility** and **capability** to tackle any challenge in today's cross-platform world.

27

Chapter 2

Setting Up a Modern Development Environment

To begin building **cross-platform applications** using **Python and C#**, it's essential to have the **right development environment**. This chapter walks you through the **setup process** for both **Python** and **C#**, providing you with the necessary tools, **IDEs**, and **version control** practices that are essential for **modern application development**.

2.1 Installing and Configuring Python and C# Development Tools

Installing Python Development Tools

1. **Download and Install Python**
   - o Go to the official Python website: Python.org
   - o Download the latest version of **Python 3.x** for your operating system (Windows, macOS, Linux).

o During installation, ensure the option **"Add Python to PATH"** is selected for easy access via command line.

2. Installing Python Libraries

o Use **pip** (Python's package installer) to install additional libraries and frameworks.

o Open a terminal (Command Prompt or terminal for macOS/Linux) and use the following command to install a package:

```sh

pip install <package-name>
```

3. Setting Up Virtual Environments (Optional but recommended)

o Virtual environments help isolate dependencies for each project, preventing version conflicts between libraries.

```sh

python -m venv myenv
source myenv/bin/activate    # On Windows: myenv\Scripts\activate
```

4. Installing Python IDE/Editor

29

o To write and run Python code, you need a good IDE or editor, which we will discuss next.

Installing C# Development Tools

1. Download and Install .NET SDK

o Go to the official **.NET website**: dotnet.microsoft.com

o Download and install the **.NET SDK** for your operating system (Windows, macOS, Linux).

2. Installing .NET Core Runtime (Optional)

o If you only need to run a .NET application (without development), you can install just the runtime.

3. Installing C# IDE

o You'll need an IDE or code editor that supports C#. **Visual Studio** and **JetBrains Rider** are popular choices.

o Once installed, you can create your first **C# project** by running:

```sh

dotnet new console -n MyFirstApp
cd MyFirstApp
dotnet run
```

2.2 Best IDEs: Visual Studio, VS Code, PyCharm, JetBrains Rider

Choosing the right **IDE** or **code editor** can significantly improve your productivity. Below are the best IDEs and editors for **Python** and **C#** development.

Python IDEs and Editors

1. **PyCharm**

    o **PyCharm** is one of the most **popular IDEs** for Python development, providing advanced features like **code completion, error checking, refactoring**, and **debugging**.

    o There are **two versions**:

        ▪ **PyCharm Community Edition**: Free and open-source.

        ▪ **PyCharm Professional Edition**: Paid version with advanced features, including support for **web frameworks** (Django, Flask).

    o You can download PyCharm from the official website: JetBrains PyCharm.

31

2. VS Code

- o **Visual Studio Code** is a lightweight, **cross-platform code editor** with Python support via extensions.
- o Install the **Python extension** from the marketplace for features like **syntax highlighting, linting,** and **IntelliSense**.
- o Highly customizable and supports many languages via plugins.
- o Download from: VS Code

3. Jupyter Notebooks

- o If you're into **data science, Jupyter** is one of the best tools for **interactive coding**. It allows you to write Python code in **notebooks**, ideal for data analysis and visualization.
- o Install via:

```sh
```

```
pip install notebook
```

C# IDEs and Editors

1. Visual Studio

- o **Visual Studio** is the **most feature-rich** IDE for **C# and .NET** development.

o Provides tools for **debugging, profiling**, and **unit testing**.

o Supports **cross-platform** development via **.NET Core**, and you can also create web, mobile, and desktop applications.

o Available for **Windows** and **macOS** (Visual Studio for Mac).

o Download from: Visual Studio

2. **JetBrains Rider**

o **JetBrains Rider** is a powerful, **cross-platform IDE for .NET, C#, and ASP.NET** development.

o Provides **smart code completion**, **refactoring tools**, and **advanced debugging** capabilities.

o Rider is based on **IntelliJ IDEA**, so if you're familiar with JetBrains tools, Rider is an excellent choice.

o Download from: JetBrains Rider

3. **VS Code** (For C#)

o **Visual Studio Code** is also a great editor for **C#** development when paired with the **C# extension**.

o Lightweight and extensible, it works well for those who want something simpler than Visual Studio.

2.3 Version Control with Git and GitHub

Version control is crucial in modern software development to track changes, collaborate with other developers, and manage multiple versions of your codebase.

Installing Git

1. Download **Git** from: Git
2. After installation, you can verify it by typing:

```sh
```

```
git --version
```

Setting Up a Git Repository

1. **Initialize a new Git repository** in your project directory:

```sh
```

```
git init
```

2. **Stage files** for commit:

```sh
```

```
git add .
```

3. **Commit the changes**:

```sh
```

```
git commit -m "Initial commit"
```

4. **Create a GitHub repository**:
    - o   Go to **GitHub**, create a new repository, and the **repository URL**.
    - o   Link your local repository to GitHub:

```sh
```

```
git       remote      add       origin
https://github.com/yourusername/you
r-repository.git
```

5. **Push changes** to GitHub:

```sh
```

```
git push -u origin master
```

GitHub for Collaboration

- GitHub allows you to **collaborate with other developers**. Features like **pull requests, branching**, and **issue tracking** make it easy to manage code in teams.
- Developers can **fork repositories, submit pull requests**, and **review code** collaboratively.

Conclusion

By setting up the right development tools for both **Python and C#**, you will be equipped to build **cross-platform applications** efficiently. Whether you're working on **web development, AI, mobile apps, or cloud solutions**, the IDEs, tools, and version control systems discussed in this chapter will serve as the foundation for modern, productive development.

Now that you have your development environment set up, you're ready to **begin building** your first cross-platform application with Python and C#. In the next chapter, we'll dive into **cross-platform development best practices**, enabling you to write applications that seamlessly run across

multiple platforms without compromising performance or user experience.

Chapter 3

Understanding Python and C#: Strengths and Differences

In this chapter, we will explore the **key differences** between **Python** and **C#**, two of the most popular and versatile programming languages used in modern application development. We will discuss their **flexibility vs. structure**, **typing systems**, and **performance considerations**, providing insight into **which language to choose** depending on the needs of your project.

3.1 How Python's Flexibility Compares to C#'s Structure

One of the first differences between **Python** and **C#** is their **design philosophy**. Python is known for its **flexibility**, while C# is more **structured and robust**, especially for large-scale applications. Let's break down these differences:

Python's Flexibility

- **Dynamic Typing**: Python is a **dynamically typed** language, meaning you don't need to explicitly declare variable types. This makes Python incredibly flexible and allows for **faster prototyping** and more **concise code**.

  python

  ```
  x = 5  # No type declaration needed
  x = "Hello"  # Reassigning to a string is valid
  ```

- **Minimal Syntax**: Python's syntax is often described as **"clean"** and **"readable"**. It uses indentation to define blocks of code instead of curly braces or other delimiters, making it intuitive and easy for beginners to learn.

  python

  ```
  def greet(name):
      print(f"Hello, {name}")
  ```

- **High-level abstractions**: Python's standard library provides high-level abstractions and powerful

39

modules, such as **Django** for web development and **TensorFlow** for machine learning, making it ideal for a variety of applications without needing deep knowledge of low-level programming concepts.

C#'s Structure

- **Static Typing**: C# is a **statically typed** language, meaning you must explicitly declare the data types of variables and parameters at compile time. This provides **strong type safety**, **early error detection**, and enhanced **IDE support** for autocompletion and debugging.

csharp

```
int x = 5;  // Explicit type declaration
x = "Hello";  // This will result in a
compile-time error
```

- **Object-Oriented**: C# is a **pure object-oriented language** (though it supports **functional programming**), meaning everything is treated as an object. This structure is beneficial when creating large-scale, maintainable systems.

csharp

```
public class Car
{
    public string Model { get; set; }
    public       void       Drive()        {
Console.WriteLine("Driving"); }
}
```

- **Explicit Class and Method Definitions**: C# requires a more **structured approach** to defining classes, methods, and properties, which adds overhead but enhances **code readability** and **maintainability** in large teams or projects.

3.2 Typing Systems: Dynamic vs. Static

One of the most fundamental differences between Python and C# lies in their **typing systems**. Understanding how dynamic and static typing affect development and performance is crucial when choosing between the two.

41

Dynamic Typing in Python

- **Dynamic Typing** means that variable types are determined at **runtime**, and you don't need to specify them when declaring variables or function parameters. Python is very flexible in this regard, allowing developers to change the type of a variable during execution.

  o **Advantages**:

    - **Faster prototyping**: Python allows you to quickly test ideas and iterate through solutions.

    - **Less boilerplate code**: You don't have to declare types or create type hierarchies.

    - **Less restrictive**: Variables can change types, which makes it easier to work with unknown or fluctuating data types.

  o **Disadvantages**:

    - **Run-time errors**: Errors related to types are only discovered during execution, which can lead to bugs that are harder to detect and debug.

    - **Reduced optimization**: Since types are resolved at runtime, Python cannot optimize performance as effectively as statically typed languages.

```python
def add(a, b):
    return a + b   # No need for type
annotations
```

Static Typing in C#

- **Static Typing** means that variable types must be explicitly defined at **compile time**, and you can't change the type of a variable once it's declared.

  o **Advantages**:

    ▪ **Compile-time error checking**: Errors related to incorrect types are caught early in the development cycle, reducing bugs during runtime.

    ▪ **Performance optimization**: Static typing allows compilers to optimize the code more efficiently, as it knows the exact types and their constraints.

    ▪ **Better tooling**: IDEs like **Visual Studio** offer excellent support for **refactoring**, **autocompletion**, and **code navigation** because of the explicit type definitions.

43

- ○ **Disadvantages**:
  - **More code**: You must explicitly define types for variables and function parameters, which can lead to more **verbose code**.
  - **Less flexibility**: You can't change types on the fly, which might make some use cases more complicated.

```csharp
public int Add(int a, int b)
{
    return a + b;  // Types are explicitly defined
}
```

3.3 Performance Considerations: When to Choose Python or C#

Both Python and C# are **high-level programming languages**, but they offer different **performance characteristics** that can significantly impact the choice of language for your project.

Python's Performance

- **Interpreter-based**: Python is an **interpreted** language, meaning that code is executed line-by-line by the **Python interpreter** at runtime. This generally leads to **slower performance** compared to compiled languages like C#.

- **Global Interpreter Lock (GIL)**: Python's GIL makes it challenging to execute **multi-threaded** code on multiple CPU cores in parallel. This means that Python can be less performant for **CPU-bound tasks** that need true parallelism.

- **Best Use Cases**:
  - **Scripting and automation**: Python is ideal for small scripts or automation tasks where speed is less critical.
  - **Data science and machine learning**: Libraries like **NumPy** and **TensorFlow** often **offload computation to C** under the hood, providing **high performance** despite Python's inherent limitations.
  - **Web development**: Python's flexibility and frameworks like **Django** make it great for quick web app development, but you might not use it

for extremely high-traffic, performance-sensitive applications.

- **Optimizing Python Performance**: Although Python is generally slower than C#, tools like **Cython**, **PyPy**, and **Numba** can optimize Python performance, especially for computation-heavy tasks.

C#'s Performance

- **Compiled Language**: C# is a **compiled language**, which means that the code is first **translated into machine code** before it is run. This typically leads to **better performance** compared to interpreted languages like Python.
- **JIT Compilation**: C# uses **Just-In-Time (JIT)** compilation, which means it compiles to native code at runtime. While it does introduce some overhead, it allows for **runtime optimizations**.
- **Multi-threading and Parallelism**: C# is designed to support **multi-threading** and **parallel programming** out-of-the-box, with features like **async/await** and the **Task Parallel Library** (TPL). This allows C# to efficiently utilize multi-core processors for computationally intensive tasks.

46

- **Best Use Cases**:
  - o **Enterprise applications**: C# is ideal for building **large-scale, high-performance, and mission-critical applications**, especially when coupled with the **.NET Core** framework.
  - o **Game development**: C# is widely used in **Unity** for building cross-platform games due to its **performance** and **rich toolset**.
  - o **High-performance backends**: With features like **ASP.NET Core**, C# can handle large-scale, high-performance web services.

- **Optimizing C# Performance**: C# is highly optimized for performance, but developers can fine-tune their applications by utilizing **memory management tools, threading**, and **native libraries** for performance-critical tasks.

3.4 When to Choose Python vs. C#

Choose Python when:

- You need to quickly develop and prototype a project.

- The focus is on **data science, machine learning**, or **automation scripts**.
- You are working with **rapid development frameworks** for web apps (e.g., Django, Flask).
- The project involves **data-heavy tasks** where performance can be offloaded to optimized libraries.

Choose C# when:

- You are building **enterprise-level applications** that require **scalability** and **robust performance**.
- You need to develop **cross-platform applications** (desktop, mobile, web) with a unified codebase using **.NET Core** or **Xamarin**.
- The project is **game development**, especially with **Unity**.
- You need **high-performance backends**, particularly for **web services** using **ASP.NET Core**.

Conclusion

Both **Python** and **C#** offer unique strengths that can be leveraged depending on your project requirements. **Python** excels in **flexibility** and rapid development, making it a great choice for prototyping, data science, and automation. On the other hand, **C#** shines in **structured, performance-critical applications**, especially when dealing with large-scale enterprise solutions, cloud computing, and game development.

By understanding these **core differences**, you will be better equipped to choose the right tool for the job, ensuring that your application meets both **functional and performance requirements**.

Part 2

Mastering Cross-Platform Development

Chapter 4

Writing Cross-Platform Applications: Best Practices

In today's world of **multi-platform applications**, it is essential to write code that can run seamlessly on different operating systems, including **Windows**, **macOS**, and **Linux**. Both **Python** and **C#** provide powerful tools and frameworks to enable developers to build cross-platform applications. In this chapter, we will dive into best practices for writing applications that work across different platforms, **understand platform dependencies**, and help you choose the **right frameworks** to use in your projects.

4.1 Developing Windows, macOS, and Linux Apps with Python and C#

1. Python Cross-Platform Development

Python's **cross-platform nature** allows you to write code that works on all major operating systems without

51

modification. However, you must be aware of platform-specific dependencies that might affect how your application runs. Here's how to approach cross-platform development with Python:

- **Use cross-platform libraries**: Many Python libraries support all major platforms, but some libraries may rely on platform-specific implementations.
- **Ensure compatibility**: Always test your application on each target platform (Windows, macOS, Linux) to ensure there are no OS-specific bugs or issues.
- **Avoid hardcoded file paths**: Since file system paths vary between operating systems (e.g., `c:\` on Windows, `/usr/` on Linux), always use the `os.path` module for file operations.

```python
python

import os
# Correct way to create a file path
file_path    =    os.path.join("data",
"myfile.txt")
```

- **Cross-platform GUI development**: Python has several libraries for building GUIs that work across platforms:
  - o **Tkinter**: The standard GUI library for Python, works on Windows, macOS, and Linux.
  - o **PyQt**: A more feature-rich library that also supports cross-platform GUI development.
  - o **Kivy**: Focuses on **multi-touch applications** and is designed for cross-platform support.

2. C# Cross-Platform Development

With the introduction of **.NET Core** and now **.NET 5 and beyond, C# has become truly cross-platform**. You can build applications that run on **Windows, macOS**, and **Linux** using **.NET Core** (now unified as the **.NET 5+** framework).

- **.NET Core/5+** is cross-platform by design, supporting not only **desktop** and **web applications** but also **mobile apps** through Xamarin and MAUI.
- **Platform-specific dependencies**: C# abstracts away many platform-specific differences, but in some cases, you may need platform-specific implementations for tasks like **file handling, networking**, and **UI design**. Always check platform-specific APIs when necessary.

Example of a cross-platform application:

- **Console applications**: C# .NET Core applications can run on all platforms without modification.

```csharp
Console.WriteLine("Hello,    Cross-Platform
World!");
```

For **cross-platform desktop** applications, use frameworks like **.NET MAUI** (discussed later).

4.2 Understanding Platform Dependencies

When writing **cross-platform applications**, it's essential to understand how dependencies differ across platforms. This can influence everything from **file management** to how the application interacts with hardware resources or the **user interface**.

1. File System Dependencies

- **Windows** uses **backslashes** (\) for file paths, whereas **macOS** and **Linux** use **forward slashes** (/).
- **File system case-sensitivity** differs:
    - **Windows**: Not case-sensitive (e.g., `File.txt` and `file.txt` are the same).
    - **macOS/Linux**: Case-sensitive by default (e.g., `File.txt` and `file.txt` are different files).

Best Practice: Always use **platform-independent** libraries like `os.path` (Python) and `Path.Combine` (C#) to handle file paths.

2. UI and User Experience

- UI design can differ significantly between platforms. For instance, **macOS** apps follow the **Cocoa** design guidelines, while **Windows** apps follow the **WinUI** design principles. **Linux** has a variety of desktop environments, such as **GNOME** and **KDE**.
- **Native look and feel**: You may need to **adapt UI components** to look native on each platform.

Best Practice: Use frameworks like **.NET MAUI** for C# or **PyQt** for Python that abstract away many of the platform-specific details and help maintain a consistent experience across platforms.

3. Performance Considerations

- Each platform may have different performance characteristics due to underlying OS differences, hardware, or available system resources.
- For example, **macOS** and **Linux** typically have better support for **multi-threading** and **parallel processing** compared to Windows (depending on configuration).

Best Practice: Test performance on all target platforms to identify potential bottlenecks or performance issues.

4.3 Choosing the Right Framework: .NET MAUI, PyQt, Kivy, Blazor

To help you develop cross-platform applications efficiently, it's important to choose the right framework. Below are some of the most popular cross-platform frameworks for both **Python** and **C#**.

1. .NET MAUI (C#)

.NET MAUI (Multi-platform App UI) is the **successor to Xamarin** and allows you to write applications for **Windows, macOS, Android, and iOS** with a single codebase.

- **Features**:
  - Supports building **native mobile, desktop, and web applications**.
  - **Unified API**: One codebase for all platforms.
  - **Integration with .NET 6+**: Leverages the full power of .NET and the ecosystem.
- **Best Use Cases**: Mobile apps (Android/iOS) and desktop apps (Windows/macOS), especially for **enterprise applications**.

Example:

csharp

```csharp
public class MainPage : ContentPage
{
    public MainPage()
    {
        var label = new Label
        {
            Text = "Hello, World!",
```

```
        VerticalOptions              =
LayoutOptions.CenterAndExpand,
        HorizontalOptions            =
LayoutOptions.CenterAndExpand
      };

      Content = label;
   }
}
```

2. PyQt (Python)

PyQt is a set of Python bindings for the **Qt application framework**, which is used to build **cross-platform desktop applications**.

- **Features**:
  - ○ **Rich UI widgets** and tools for building feature-rich applications.
  - ○ **Works on Windows, macOS, and Linux** with minimal changes.
  - ○ Extensive support for **GUI design**, including **drag-and-drop** tools like **Qt Designer**.
- **Best Use Cases**: Desktop applications with advanced user interfaces.

Example:

```
python

from   PyQt5.QtWidgets   import   QApplication,
QWidget

app = QApplication([])
window = QWidget()
window.setWindowTitle('Hello, PyQt!')
window.show()
app.exec_()
```

3. Kivy (Python)

Kivy is a **Python framework** used for developing **multi-touch applications**, especially for **mobile apps**.

- **Features**:
  - o Supports **Android, iOS, Windows, macOS**, and **Linux**.
  - o Excellent for **touch-based** or **gesture-based applications**.
  - o Easy to integrate with **native device features** (camera, sensors, etc.).
- **Best Use Cases**: Touch-based applications, mobile apps, and games.

Example:

```python
python

from kivy.app import App
from kivy.uix.label import Label

class MyApp(App):
    def build(self):
        return Label(text="Hello, Kivy!")

if __name__ == "__main__":
    MyApp().run()
```

4. Blazor (C#)

Blazor allows you to build **web applications** using **C#** instead of JavaScript. Blazor WebAssembly lets you run **C# code directly in the browser** using WebAssembly.

- **Features**:
  - o **C#-based** front-end development for web apps.
  - o **WebAssembly** support allows for running .NET code on the browser.
  - o **Strong integration with .NET** and **ASP.NET Core** for full-stack web development.
- **Best Use Cases**: Web applications where you want to write front-end logic in **C#** instead of JavaScript.

Example:

```
csharp

@page "/"

<h3>Hello, Blazor!</h3>
<p>Welcome to Blazor web development.</p>
```

4.4 Best Practices for Writing Cross-Platform Code

1. **Abstract Platform-Specific Code**: When using different platform-specific APIs, abstract the platform-dependent parts into separate modules to make your code more maintainable.

2. **Avoid Hardcoding Platform Paths**: Use platform-independent methods (e.g., `os.path.join()` in Python or `Path.Combine()` in C#) for file paths.

3. **Test on Multiple Platforms**: Always test your application on **all target platforms** to ensure compatibility and address any platform-specific issues early in the development cycle.

4. **Responsive and Adaptive UIs**: Make sure that the user interface adjusts correctly to different screen

sizes, resolutions, and form factors, especially for mobile devices.

Conclusion

Writing **cross-platform applications** requires careful consideration of platform-specific nuances, but with the right tools and frameworks, you can develop applications that work seamlessly across **Windows, macOS**, and **Linux**. Whether you're working with **Python or C#**, tools like **.NET MAUI, PyQt, Kivy**, and **Blazor** allow you to build scalable, robust, and modern applications with ease.

In the next chapter, we will explore the **best practices for backend development** and how you can effectively build **RESTful APIs** with **Python** and **C#**, making your cross-platform apps more powerful and dynamic.

Let's continue building!

Chapter 5

GUI Development with Python and C#

Graphical User Interface (GUI) development is crucial for **desktop applications**, as it defines how users interact with your software. In this chapter, we will explore how to build **cross-platform desktop applications** using **Python** and **C#** with popular frameworks like **Tkinter, PyQt, WPF**, and **MAUI**. We will also discuss the differences between **native UI** and **web-based UI**, and we will walk through a **real-world example** of creating a **multi-platform to-do list app**.

5.1 Building Desktop Applications with Tkinter, PyQt, WPF, and MAUI

1. Tkinter (Python)

Tkinter is the **standard Python library** for building simple desktop applications. It's lightweight and comes bundled with most Python installations, making it a great choice for **quick prototypes** or simple desktop tools.

- **Features**:
  - o Lightweight and built-in with Python, so no extra installations are needed.
  - o Simple, easy-to-understand API.
  - o Works on **Windows, macOS**, and **Linux**.
- **Creating a simple window**:

```python
import tkinter as tk

root = tk.Tk()   # Create the main window
root.title("To-Do List")

label   =   tk.Label(root,   text="Hello,
Tkinter!")
label.pack()   # Add the label to the window

root.mainloop()   # Start the GUI event loop
```

- **Best Use Case**: Suitable for **lightweight applications** like simple **form-based apps** or utilities.

2. PyQt (Python)

PyQt is a set of **Python bindings** for the **Qt application framework**, which is powerful enough to create more complex desktop applications with rich UIs.

- **Features**:
  - Highly **feature-rich**, supporting advanced widgets like **tables, charts**, and **tree views**.
  - Cross-platform support for **Windows, macOS, and Linux**.
  - Integrates with **Qt Designer** for **drag-and-drop UI design**.
- **Example: Creating a To-Do List App**:

```python
python

from PyQt5.QtWidgets import QApplication,
QWidget,    QVBoxLayout,    QPushButton,
QListWidget

app = QApplication([])    # Create the
application

window = QWidget()
window.setWindowTitle("To-Do List")

layout = QVBoxLayout()
```

```
list_widget = QListWidget()
layout.addWidget(list_widget)

button = QPushButton("Add Task")
layout.addWidget(button)

button.clicked.connect(lambda:
list_widget.addItem("New Task"))

window.setLayout(layout)
window.show()

app.exec_()   # Run the application
```

- **Best Use Case**: Ideal for building **complex UIs** and apps that require **advanced widgets** (e.g., file managers, media players).

3. WPF (C#)

Windows Presentation Foundation (WPF) is one of the most widely used frameworks for building **rich desktop applications** in **C#**.

- **Features**:
  - Built specifically for **Windows**.

66

- o Rich support for **data-binding**, **templates**, and **animations**.

- o Deep integration with the **Windows OS** and **.NET ecosystem**.

- **Example: Creating a To-Do List App**:

```xml
xml

<Window x:Class="ToDoApp.MainWindow"

xmlns="http://schemas.microsoft.com/winfx
/2006/xaml/presentation"

xmlns:x="http://schemas.microsoft.com/win
fx/2006/xaml"
        Title="To-Do    List"   Height="350"
Width="525">
    <Grid>
        <ListBox        Name="taskListBox"
VerticalAlignment="Top" Height="200"/>
        <Button    Content="Add     Task"
VerticalAlignment="Bottom" Click="AddTask"
/>
    </Grid>
</Window>
```

```csharp
csharp

using System.Windows;
```

```
namespace ToDoApp
{
    public partial class MainWindow :
Window
    {
        public MainWindow()
        {
            InitializeComponent();
        }

        private void AddTask(object
sender, RoutedEventArgs e)
        {
            taskListBox.Items.Add("New
Task");
        }
    }
}
```

- **Best Use Case**: **Windows-only** desktop applications with **rich UIs,** like **business applications** or **media players**.

4. .NET MAUI (C#)

.NET MAUI (Multi-platform App UI) is a cross-platform framework for building apps that run on **Windows, macOS, Android, and iOS** using a single codebase.

- **Features**:
  - Supports multiple platforms (**Windows, macOS, iOS, Android**).
  - **Unified codebase** for all platforms.
  - Deep integration with **.NET** and **XAML** for UI design.

- **Example: Creating a To-Do List App**:

```csharp
public class MainPage : ContentPage
{
    public MainPage()
    {
        var listView = new ListView();
        listView.Items.Add("New Task");

        var addButton = new Button
        {
            Text = "Add Task"
        };
        addButton.Clicked    +=    (sender, args) =>
        {
            listView.Items.Add("Another Task");
        };
```

69

```
Content = new StackLayout
{
        Children    =    {    listView,
addButton }
        };
    }
}
```

- **Best Use Case**: **Cross-platform mobile and desktop apps** where a **single codebase** is required for both **mobile devices** and **desktop operating systems**.

5.2 Comparing Native UI vs. Web-Based UI

As applications become more **cross-platform**, developers must decide whether to use a **native UI** or a **web-based UI**. Both approaches have their advantages and trade-offs.

Native UI

- **Advantages**:

- o **Performance**: Native applications generally offer **better performance** since they interact directly with the underlying operating system.
- o **Platform-specific features**: Native UI frameworks can make use of **system-level features** (e.g., **notifications, system tray, native UI controls**).
- o **Seamless user experience**: Native applications feel **integrated with the OS**, offering a more **consistent experience** for users.

- **Disadvantages**:
  - o **Platform-specific code**: While frameworks like **.NET MAUI, PyQt**, and **Kivy** help with cross-platform development, developers still have to account for platform-specific quirks and dependencies.
  - o **Larger application size**: Native applications tend to be larger in size compared to web-based apps.

Web-Based UI

- **Advantages**:
  - o **Cross-platform compatibility**: Web applications can run on **any platform** with a web browser, making them incredibly flexible.

71

- o **Easier updates**: Updating a web app is as simple as changing the code on the server, without needing to push updates to users.
- o **Accessibility**: Web applications are accessible from any device with a **web browser**, which is ideal for **SaaS** or **enterprise applications**.

- **Disadvantages**:
  - o **Performance**: Web apps can't always match the performance of native apps, especially when dealing with **heavy UI rendering** or **hardware-intensive tasks**.
  - o **Internet dependency**: Web applications typically require a **stable internet connection** to work, though **Progressive Web Apps (PWAs)** are changing that.

Best Use Case for Native UI: When building apps that require **high performance**, access to **native OS features**, and a **consistent look-and-feel** (e.g., desktop apps, mobile apps, media applications).

Best Use Case for Web-Based UI: When building apps that are **highly accessible**, require **easy maintenance**, or need to run **on multiple devices** with minimal installation (e.g., **SaaS, web apps, admin dashboards**).

5.3 Real-World Example: Creating a Multi-Platform To-Do List App

1. Design Overview

We will create a **simple to-do list application** that works across **Windows, macOS**, and **Linux**. The application will include:

- A **list view** to display tasks.
- A **button** to add new tasks.

We'll create the app using **Python with Tkinter** and **C# with .NET MAUI** to compare the two approaches.

2. Python Version (Tkinter)

python

```python
import tkinter as tk

class ToDoApp:
    def __init__(self, root):
        self.root = root
        self.root.title("To-Do List")
```

73

```python
        self.task_listbox                =
tk.Listbox(self.root)
        self.task_listbox.pack(fill=tk.BOTH,
expand=True)

        self.add_button  =  tk.Button(self.root,
text="Add Task", command=self.add_task)
        self.add_button.pack()

    def add_task(self):
        task = "New Task"
        self.task_listbox.insert(tk.END, task)

if __name__ == "__main__":
    root = tk.Tk()
    app = ToDoApp(root)
    root.mainloop()
```

3. C# Version (.NET MAUI)

csharp

```csharp
using Microsoft.Maui.Controls;

public class MainPage : ContentPage
{
    public MainPage()
    {
        var listView = new ListView();
        listView.Items.Add("New Task");
```

```
var addButton = new Button
{
    Text = "Add Task"
};
addButton.Clicked += (sender, args) =>
{
    listView.Items.Add("Another Task");
};

Content = new StackLayout
{
    Children = { listView, addButton }
};
    }
}
```

Conclusion

In this chapter, we explored how to develop cross-platform desktop applications using **Python** and **C#**, focusing on frameworks such as **Tkinter, PyQt, WPF**, and **.NET MAUI**. We also discussed the trade-offs between **native UI** and **web-based UI**, helping you decide which approach is best for your application. Finally, we walked through a real-world example of creating a **multi-platform to-do list app**, demonstrating how these tools can be used to build applications that run smoothly on **Windows, macOS**, and **Linux**.

In the next chapter, we'll dive into **backend development** and **RESTful API creation** with both Python and C#, further extending the functionality of our cross-platform applications.

Let's continue building!

Chapter 6

Web Development: Python Django vs. C# ASP.NET Core

Web development is a key area where Python and C# excel, but the choice between **Django**, **Flask**, and **ASP.NET Core** depends on the specific needs of your application. In this chapter, we will compare the **Python web frameworks** (**Django** and **Flask**) with **C#'s ASP.NET Core**, explore **deployment** on major cloud platforms like **Azure**, **AWS**, and **Google Cloud**, and dive into **full-stack development** with **Blazor** and **React**.

6.1 When to Choose Django or Flask vs. ASP.NET Core

Choosing between **Python** and **C#** for web development often comes down to the specific needs of your project, team expertise, and long-term goals. Let's look at **Django**, **Flask**, and **ASP.NET Core** to see when each is the best fit.

1. Django (Python)

Django is a **high-level web framework** for building **full-featured web applications** quickly and efficiently.

- **Key Features**:
    - **Batteries-included**: Django comes with built-in features such as **authentication, admin panel, ORM (Object-Relational Mapping)**, and more. It's perfect for building **robust and scalable web apps** with less configuration.
    - **Convention over configuration**: Django enforces a standard structure, which leads to **consistency** across applications.
    - **Security**: Django has built-in protection against **CSRF, SQL injection**, and other common web vulnerabilities.
- **Best Use Cases**:
    - **Rapid development of data-driven applications**.
    - Large applications where you need a **ready-to-go** solution with minimal setup.
    - Ideal for building **content management systems, social media platforms**, and **e-commerce sites**.
- **When to Choose Django**:

o If you are looking for an **all-in-one solution** that provides the core components of a web app out of the box.

o If your team is familiar with Python and you want to take advantage of Python's libraries for data analysis, machine learning, or AI.

Example:

python

```
# Django view
from django.http import HttpResponse
def hello(request):
    return HttpResponse("Hello, World!")
```

2. Flask (Python)

Flask is a **lightweight web framework** that offers more flexibility compared to Django, giving you the ability to **build web applications from scratch**.

- **Key Features**:
  o **Minimalist design**: Flask gives you the bare essentials, allowing you to pick and choose the libraries and tools you need.

- **Highly customizable**: Great for developers who need flexibility and want to control how their web application is structured.
- **Simple to learn**: Flask's simplicity makes it ideal for beginners and small projects.

- **Best Use Cases**:
  - **Small to medium-sized applications**.
  - APIs, microservices, and applications that don't require a complex, full-stack framework.
  - Projects where you need **flexibility** and want to hand-pick your tools.

- **When to Choose Flask**:
  - If you need a **lightweight solution** and want full control over your project structure.
  - If you're building **small applications, RESTful APIs**, or **prototypes**.

Example:

python

```
from flask import Flask
app = Flask(__name__)

@app.route('/')
def hello():
    return "Hello, Flask!"
```

80

```
if __name__ == '__main__':
    app.run()
```

3. ASP.NET Core (C#)

ASP.NET Core is a **cross-platform, high-performance framework** for building **modern web applications** and APIs using C#.

- **Key Features**:
  - **Cross-platform**: ASP.NET Core runs on **Windows, macOS**, and **Linux**.
  - **High performance**: ASP.NET Core is one of the **fastest web frameworks**, optimized for **high-traffic applications**.
  - **Modular architecture**: You can use **just the components you need** and add features as required, allowing for efficient and maintainable code.
- **Best Use Cases**:
  - **Enterprise-level applications**, especially for organizations that already rely on the **Microsoft ecosystem** (e.g., Azure, SQL Server).
  - **Highly scalable APIs** and **high-performance web applications**.
  - **Cloud-based applications** built with **.NET**.

81

- **When to Choose ASP.NET Core**:
  - If you're working with **C#** and **Microsoft technologies** (e.g., **Azure**).
  - If you need **high performance** and **scalability** for your web applications and APIs.

Example:

csharp

```
// ASP.NET Core controller
public class HelloController : Controller
{
    public IActionResult Index()
    {
        return    Content("Hello,    ASP.NET
Core!");
    }
}
```

6.2 Deploying Web Apps on Azure, AWS, and Google Cloud

Now that you have your **Python** or **C#** web app, the next step is to **deploy** it to the cloud. We will cover how to deploy applications to three of the most popular cloud platforms: **Azure**, **AWS**, and **Google Cloud**.

1. Deploying to Azure

Azure is **Microsoft's cloud platform** and is tightly integrated with the **.NET ecosystem**, making it a natural choice for deploying **ASP.NET Core** applications.

- **Deploying ASP.NET Core to Azure**:
  - **Azure App Service** is a fully managed platform for deploying **web applications**.
  - Use **GitHub Actions** or **Azure DevOps** to set up **CI/CD pipelines**.
  - Azure also offers **Azure SQL Database** for relational storage and **Azure Blob Storage** for unstructured data.

  Example:

```bash
az webapp create --resource-group
MyResourceGroup --plan MyAppServicePlan --
name MyAppName --runtime "DOTNETCORE|3.1"
```

2. Deploying to AWS

AWS offers a wide variety of services, with **Elastic Beanstalk** being one of the easiest ways to deploy **Python** and **C#** web applications.

- **Deploying Django or Flask on AWS**:
    - o Use **Elastic Beanstalk** to deploy **Django** or **Flask** applications quickly.
    - o AWS also supports **RDS** for relational databases and **S3** for storage.

  Example:

  bash

  ```
  eb init -p python-3.7 my-flask-app
  eb create my-flask-app-env
  eb deploy
  ```

3. Deploying to Google Cloud

Google Cloud offers services for deploying both **Python** and **C#** applications through **Google App Engine** or **Google Kubernetes Engine (GKE)**.

- **Deploying Python/Flask to Google Cloud**:

84

o Use **Google Cloud Storage** for file storage and **Cloud SQL** for databases.

o **Google Kubernetes Engine** (GKE) is an excellent choice if you need **containerized applications**.

Example:

bash

gcloud app deploy

6.3 Full-Stack Development with Blazor and React

Blazor and **React** are powerful tools for full-stack development. While **React** is a widely used **JavaScript framework** for building web applications, **Blazor** allows you to build interactive web apps using **C#** instead of JavaScript.

1. Blazor (C#)

Blazor is a **.NET framework** that enables you to build interactive **web apps** using **C#** instead of JavaScript. Blazor can run in the **browser** using **WebAssembly** or on the **server** via SignalR.

- **Advantages**:
  - ○ **C# for both frontend and backend** development.
  - ○ **Code sharing** between client and server, making development more unified.
  - ○ **High performance** with **WebAssembly**.
- **Best Use Case**: When you want to use **C#** across both the **front-end** and **back-end** of your web application.

Example (Blazor component):

```csharp
@page "/counter"

<h3>Counter</h3>

<p>Current count: @count</p>

<button          @onclick="IncrementCount">Click
me</button>

@code {
    private int count = 0;
```

```
private void IncrementCount()
{
    count++;
}
}
```

2. React (JavaScript)

React is a **JavaScript library** for building user interfaces, particularly for **single-page applications** (SPAs).

- **Advantages**:
  - o **Declarative syntax** for UI components.
  - o **Rich ecosystem** with tools like **React Router** and **Redux** for state management.
  - o Huge community and support for various libraries and third-party tools.
- **Best Use Case**: For building **interactive, dynamic web UIs** and when you need to **work with JavaScript** on the frontend.

Example (React component):

```javascript
import React, { useState } from 'react';

function Counter() {
```

```
const [count, setCount] = useState(0);

const increment = () => setCount(count + 1);

return (
  <div>
    <h3>Counter</h3>
    <p>Current count: {count}</p>
    <button          onClick={increment}>Click
me</button>
    </div>
  );
}

export default Counter;
```

Conclusion

In this chapter, we compared **Django**, **Flask**, and **ASP.NET Core** to understand the best use cases for each framework when building web applications. We also explored how to deploy web applications to **Azure**, **AWS**, and **Google Cloud**, and how to use frameworks like **Blazor** and **React** for **full-stack development**.

Understanding when and how to use these frameworks and deployment options will help you create **robust, scalable**, and **cross-platform web applications** that can be deployed and accessed globally.

In the next chapter, we will dive into **backend development** best practices and how to integrate **APIs** into your cross-platform applications.

Let's continue the journey!

Part 3

Backend Development and

APIs

Chapter 7

Building RESTful APIs with Python (FastAPI) and C# (ASP.NET)

In this chapter, we will focus on **building RESTful APIs** with **Python** and **C#**. APIs (Application Programming Interfaces) are essential in modern web development, enabling communication between **frontend applications**, **mobile apps**, and **backend systems**. We'll dive into the concepts of **RESTful APIs** and **GraphQL**, compare them, and then proceed with a hands-on project to build a **cross-platform API** using **Python** and **C#**. Lastly, we'll explore **authentication techniques** with **JWT** and **OAuth** to secure our APIs.

7.1 Introduction to REST and GraphQL APIs

1. RESTful APIs

REST (Representational State Transfer) is an architectural style for designing networked applications. It is based on **stateless** communication where the server provides resources identified by URLs and the client interacts with these resources through standard HTTP methods.

- **Key Concepts**:
  - **Resources**: Data entities exposed via URLs (e.g., `/users`, `/posts`).
  - **HTTP Methods**:
    - **GET**: Retrieve data.
    - **POST**: Create new resources.
    - **PUT**: Update existing resources.
    - **DELETE**: Remove resources.
  - **Stateless**: Each request from the client must contain all the information needed to process it. The server does not store any session information between requests.
- **Advantages**:
  - Simple and easy to implement.
  - Wide adoption and extensive support across technologies.
  - Supports **scalable** systems.

- **Example**: A simple RESTful API endpoint in Python (FastAPI):

```python
from fastapi import FastAPI

app = FastAPI()

@app.get("/items/{item_id}")
def read_item(item_id: int, q: str = None):
    return {"item_id": item_id, "q": q}
```

2. GraphQL APIs

GraphQL is a query language for APIs developed by **Facebook** that allows clients to request exactly the data they need. Unlike REST, GraphQL exposes a **single endpoint** for accessing various resources, and the client can specify the shape of the response.

- **Key Concepts**:
    - **Single endpoint**: A GraphQL API has only one endpoint for all requests (e.g., `/graphql`).
    - **Querying**: Clients can query for only the specific fields they need, reducing over-fetching of data.
    - **Mutations**: Used for creating, updating, or deleting resources.

93

- o **Subscriptions**: Allows clients to subscribe to real-time updates.
- **Advantages**:
  - o Fine-grained control over the data returned by the API.
  - o Reduced number of requests, as clients can fetch multiple resources in a single query.
  - o Strong **type system** with automatic schema generation.
- **Example**: A simple GraphQL query for getting user data:

```graphql
query {
  user(id: "1") {
    name
    email
  }
}
```

7.2 Hands-on Project: Creating a Cross-Platform API with Python & C#

In this section, we will create a **basic RESTful API** that supports **CRUD operations** (Create, Read, Update, Delete) using both **Python (FastAPI)** and **C# (ASP.NET Core)**. This API will allow us to manage a list of **items** with attributes such as `name` and `description`.

1. Python (FastAPI) API

FastAPI is a modern Python web framework that is designed for building **high-performance APIs**. It is easy to set up and provides automatic **documentation** using **Swagger UI**.

- **Install FastAPI and Uvicorn** (ASGI server):

  bash

  ```
  pip install fastapi uvicorn
  ```

- **Define the FastAPI API**:

  python

  ```
  from fastapi import FastAPI
  from pydantic import BaseModel

  app = FastAPI()
  ```

```python
# Define data model for items
class Item(BaseModel):
    name: str
    description: str

# In-memory storage for items
items = []

@app.post("/items/")
def create_item(item: Item):
    items.append(item)
    return item

@app.get("/items/{item_id}")
def read_item(item_id: int):
    return items[item_id]

@app.put("/items/{item_id}")
def update_item(item_id: int, item: Item):
    items[item_id] = item
    return item

@app.delete("/items/{item_id}")
def delete_item(item_id: int):
    deleted_item = items.pop(item_id)
    return deleted_item

# To run the server: uvicorn main:app --
reload
```

- **Run the server**:

```bash
bash
```

```bash
uvicorn main:app --reload
```

Visit **http://localhost:8000/docs** to view the automatically generated **Swagger UI** for testing the API.

2. C# (ASP.NET Core) API

ASP.NET Core is a high-performance, cross-platform framework for building **modern web APIs** with **C#**.

- **Create a new ASP.NET Core Web API project**:
  - o Using **Visual Studio** or the **command line**, create a new API project:

```bash
bash
```

```bash
dotnet new webapi -n ItemsApi
cd ItemsApi
```

- **Define the Model and Controller**:
  - o **Item Model**:

```csharp
csharp
```

97

```csharp
public class Item
{
    public string Name { get; set; }
    public string Description { get;
set; }
}
```

o **Item Controller**:

csharp

```csharp
using Microsoft.AspNetCore.Mvc;
using System.Collections.Generic;

[Route("api/[controller]")]
[ApiController]
public   class   ItemsController   :
ControllerBase
{
    private  static  List<Item>  items
= new List<Item>();

    [HttpPost]
    public            IActionResult
CreateItem([FromBody] Item item)
    {
        items.Add(item);
```

```csharp
        return
CreatedAtAction(nameof(GetItem), new
{ id = items.Count - 1 }, item);
    }


    [HttpGet("{id}")]
    public          ActionResult<Item>
GetItem(int id)
    {
        if (id < 0 || id >=
items.Count)
            return NotFound();
        return items[id];
    }


    [HttpPut("{id}")]
    public            IActionResult
UpdateItem(int id, [FromBody] Item
item)
    {
        if (id < 0 || id >=
items.Count)
            return NotFound();
        items[id] = item;
        return NoContent();
    }


    [HttpDelete("{id}")]
```

```
public                IActionResult
DeleteItem(int id)
    {
        if  (id  <  0  ||  id  >=
items.Count)
            return NotFound();
        items.RemoveAt(id);
        return NoContent();
    }
}
```

- **Run the server**:

```bash
bash
```

```
dotnet run
```

You can now access the API via **http://localhost:5000/items** and use tools like **Postman** to interact with the API.

7.3 Authentication with JWT and OAuth

Securing your APIs is critical to ensuring that only authorized users can access your resources. Two common authentication techniques are **JWT (JSON Web Token)** and **OAuth**.

1. JSON Web Token (JWT)

JWT is a compact, URL-safe token format that can be used for **authentication** and **information exchange**. The token is typically sent as part of the request header.

- **How JWT works**:
  1. The client sends a **username** and **password** to the server.
  2. If the credentials are correct, the server generates a **JWT** token and sends it back to the client.
  3. The client includes this token in the **Authorization header** of future requests.
  4. The server validates the token and grants access to the protected resource.
- **JWT Authentication Example (Python with FastAPI)**:

```python
python
```

```python
from fastapi import Depends, HTTPException
from        fastapi.security        import
OAuth2PasswordBearer
import jwt
from datetime import datetime, timedelta

oauth2_scheme                                =
OAuth2PasswordBearer(tokenUrl="token")

SECRET_KEY = "mysecretkey"

def create_access_token(data: dict):
    expire    =    datetime.utcnow()    +
timedelta(hours=1)
    to_encode = data.()
    to_encode.update({"exp": expire})
    return            jwt.encode(to_encode,
SECRET_KEY, algorithm="HS256")

def    get_current_user(token:    str    =
Depends(oauth2_scheme)):
    try:
        payload    =    jwt.decode(token,
SECRET_KEY, algorithms=["HS256"])
        return payload
    except jwt.ExpiredSignatureError:
        raise
HTTPException(status_code=401,
detail="Token expired")
```

```
except jwt.JWTError:
    raise
HTTPException(status_code=401,
detail="Invalid token")
```

2. OAuth

OAuth is an authorization protocol that allows third-party services to exchange data on behalf of a user. It's commonly used for **social logins** and **authorization**.

- **OAuth Flow**:
    1. The client redirects the user to the authorization server.
    2. The user grants permission for the client to access their data.
    3. The authorization server returns an **access token** to the client.
    4. The client uses the **access token** to make authorized API requests.
- **OAuth Example (ASP.NET Core)**: Configure **OAuth** with a third-party provider like **Google** in the **Startup.cs** class to handle authentication via OAuth.

Conclusion

In this chapter, we explored the process of building **RESTful APIs** with **Python (FastAPI)** and **C# (ASP.NET Core)**. We also discussed **authentication techniques** with **JWT** and **OAuth**, which are essential for securing your APIs. These techniques are critical for **cross-platform applications** that require user authentication and secure communication.

In the next chapter, we will dive into **database integration** and explore how to manage data in your APIs using **SQL** and **NoSQL** databases.

Let's continue building!

Chapter 8

Database Management: SQL vs. NoSQL

In this chapter, we will dive into **SQL** and **NoSQL databases**, helping you choose the right one for your project. We'll compare **PostgreSQL**, **MySQL**, and **MongoDB**, and explore how to integrate these databases with your applications using **Entity Framework** (for C#) and **SQLAlchemy** (for Python). Finally, we will build a practical example of a **cloud-connected database app** using these technologies.

8.1 Choosing the Right Database for Your Project: PostgreSQL, MySQL, MongoDB

When selecting a database for your application, you need to consider the nature of your data and the specific needs of your application. Here, we compare three popular databases—**PostgreSQL**, **MySQL**, and **MongoDB**—to help you make an informed choice.

1. SQL Databases (PostgreSQL vs. MySQL)

SQL databases use **structured query language (SQL)** for defining and manipulating data. These databases store data in **tables** with **rows and columns**, and they are often referred to as **relational databases** because the data is **related** and follows a **schema**.

- **PostgreSQL**:
    - o **Type**: Open-source, object-relational database.
    - o **Strengths**:
        - Highly **scalable**, supports **complex queries**, and has **full ACID compliance** (Atomicity, Consistency, Isolation, Durability).
        - Best for applications that require **strong consistency** and **complex relationships**.
        - **Supports JSON data types** and has extensions for **geospatial data** (PostGIS), making it a good choice for geolocation-based applications.
    - o **Use Case**: Ideal for applications that need **complex transactions, data integrity**, and **strong**

106

relational data modeling (e.g., banking systems, enterprise applications).

- **MySQL**:
  - o **Type**: Open-source relational database.
  - o **Strengths**:
    - **Faster** in certain scenarios, especially for read-heavy workloads.
    - **Widely adopted** and supported by various hosting providers, including **managed MySQL instances**.
    - Well-suited for **e-commerce** applications or smaller-scale apps that don't require extensive querying.
  - o **Use Case**: Best for **web apps, e-commerce sites**, and applications with **simple relationships** between entities.

2. NoSQL Databases (MongoDB)

NoSQL databases are designed to handle **unstructured** or **semi-structured** data, often in a **non-relational** format. These databases offer flexibility when the data model is dynamic or doesn't fit neatly into tables.

- **MongoDB**:
  - o **Type**: Document-based NoSQL database.

- ○ **Strengths**:
  - Stores data in **JSON-like documents** (BSON), which makes it flexible for handling **semi-structured data**.
  - **Scalable** and handles high-throughput applications with ease.
  - Suitable for projects that require **rapid iteration**, frequent schema changes, or working with **big data**.
- ○ **Use Case**: Ideal for **applications with evolving data models**, **real-time analytics**, or projects involving **user-generated content** (e.g., blogs, social media).

8.2 Using Entity Framework (C#) and SQLAlchemy (Python)

Once you've chosen your database, you'll need a way to interact with it. **Object-Relational Mapping (ORM)** frameworks like **Entity Framework** for C# and **SQLAlchemy** for Python allow you to interact with databases using **objects** rather than raw SQL queries.

1. Using Entity Framework (C#)

Entity Framework (EF) is a **powerful ORM** that allows C# developers to interact with databases using **C# objects**.

- **Setting Up Entity Framework in C#**:
    1. First, install the **Entity Framework Core** NuGet package:

    ```bash
    bash
    ```

    ```
    dotnet          add          package
    Microsoft.EntityFrameworkCore
    dotnet          add          package
    Microsoft.EntityFrameworkCore.SqlSe
    rver   # For SQL Server
    dotnet          add          package
    Microsoft.EntityFrameworkCore.Desig
    n   # For design-time tools
    ```

    2. Define a model class that corresponds to a table in your database:

    ```csharp
    csharp
    ```

    ```csharp
    public class Task
    {
        public int Id { get; set; }
        public string Name { get; set; }
    ```

109

```csharp
    public bool IsCompleted { get;
set; }
}
```

3. Create a **DbContext** class to manage your database operations:

csharp

```csharp
public class ApplicationDbContext :
DbContext
{
    public DbSet<Task> Tasks { get;
set; }

    protected    override    void
OnConfiguring(DbContextOptionsBuild
er optionsBuilder)
    {

optionsBuilder.UseSqlServer("YourCo
nnectionStringHere");
    }
}
```

4. Use **Migrations** to create and update the database schema:

bash

```
dotnet      ef      migrations      add
InitialCreate
dotnet ef database update
```

5. Perform basic database operations like **add**, **retrieve**, **update**, and **delete**:

```
csharp

using      (var      context      =      new
ApplicationDbContext())
{
    // Create
    var task = new Task { Name =
"Learn C#", IsCompleted = false };
    context.Tasks.Add(task);
    context.SaveChanges();

    // Read
    var                tasks                =
context.Tasks.ToList();

    // Update
    task.IsCompleted = true;
    context.SaveChanges();

    // Delete
    context.Tasks.Remove(task);
```

111

```
context.SaveChanges();
}
```

2. Using SQLAlchemy (Python)

SQLAlchemy is the most popular ORM for Python, providing a **high-level API** to interact with relational databases.

- **Setting Up SQLAlchemy in Python**:
    1. First, install **SQLAlchemy** and a database driver (e.g., **psycopg2** for PostgreSQL):

    bash

    ```
    pip install sqlalchemy psycopg2
    ```

    2. Define a model class:

    python

    ```
    from sqlalchemy import
    create_engine, Column, Integer,
    String, Boolean
    from sqlalchemy.ext.declarative
    import declarative_base
    from sqlalchemy.orm import
    sessionmaker

    Base = declarative_base()
    ```

112

```python
class Task(Base):
    __tablename__ = 'tasks'
    id        =        Column(Integer,
primary_key=True)
    name = Column(String)
    is_completed = Column(Boolean)


engine                              =
create_engine('postgresql://user:pa
ssword@localhost/mydatabase')
Base.metadata.create_all(engine)


Session = sessionmaker(bind=engine)
session = Session()
```

3. Perform database operations:

```python
python

# Create
new_task = Task(name="Learn Python",
is_completed=False)
session.add(new_task)
session.commit()

# Read
tasks = session.query(Task).all()

# Update
```

```
task                                   =
session.query(Task).filter_by(id=1)
.first()
task.is_completed = True
session.commit()

# Delete
session.delete(task)
session.commit()
```

8.3 Practical Example: Building a Cloud-Connected Database App

In this section, we will build a simple **cloud-connected to-do list application** that interacts with a database. We will use **Python (FastAPI)** with **PostgreSQL** and **C# (ASP.NET Core)** with **SQL Server** to demonstrate how to integrate databases in a cloud environment.

1. Python FastAPI with PostgreSQL

- **Create a FastAPI app** with **PostgreSQL**:

```python

from fastapi import FastAPI
```

```python
from pydantic import BaseModel
import psycopg2

app = FastAPI()

class Task(BaseModel):
    name: str
    is_completed: bool

# Database connection
conn = psycopg2.connect(
    dbname="mydb",                  user="user",
password="password", host="localhost"
)
cursor = conn.cursor()

@app.post("/tasks/")
def create_task(task: Task):
    cursor.execute("INSERT    INTO    tasks
(name,  is_completed)  VALUES  (%s,  %s)",
(task.name, task.is_completed))
    conn.commit()
    return       {"name":       task.name,
"is_completed": task.is_completed}

@app.get("/tasks/")
def read_tasks():
    cursor.execute("SELECT * FROM tasks")
    tasks = cursor.fetchall()
```

```
return tasks
```

- **Deploying the app to the cloud (e.g., AWS)**:
    o Set up a **PostgreSQL instance** on **AWS RDS** or **Heroku**.
    o Configure your app to connect to the remote database using the provided connection string.

2. C# ASP.NET Core with SQL Server

- **Create an ASP.NET Core API** with **SQL Server**:

```csharp
public class Task
{
    public int Id { get; set; }
    public string Name { get; set; }
    public bool IsCompleted { get; set; }
}

public class ApplicationDbContext : DbContext
{
    public DbSet<Task> Tasks { get; set; }

    public
ApplicationDbContext(DbContextOptions<App
licationDbContext> options)
```

116

```csharp
        : base(options) { }
}


[ApiController]
[Route("api/[controller]")]
public    class    TasksController    :
ControllerBase
{
    private readonly ApplicationDbContext
_context;

    public
TasksController(ApplicationDbContext
context)
    {
        _context = context;
    }

    [HttpPost]
    public    async    Task<IActionResult>
CreateTask([FromBody] Task task)
    {
        _context.Tasks.Add(task);
        await _context.SaveChangesAsync();
        return
CreatedAtAction(nameof(GetTask), new { id
= task.Id }, task);
    }
```

```
[HttpGet]
public     async     Task<IActionResult>
GetTasks()
    {
        var     tasks     =     await
_context.Tasks.ToListAsync();
        return Ok(tasks);
    }
}
```

- **Deploying to the cloud**:
    - o Deploy the app using **Azure App Service** or **AWS Elastic Beanstalk**.
    - o Set up a **SQL Server instance** (e.g., **Azure SQL Database**) and update the **connection string** in your application.

Conclusion

In this chapter, we learned how to choose between **SQL (PostgreSQL, MySQL)** and **NoSQL (MongoDB)** databases based on the needs of your project. We explored how to interact with these databases using **Entity Framework** (for C#) and **SQLAlchemy** (for Python). Finally, we walked through the process of building a **cloud-**

connected database app using both **Python** and **C#**, and we discussed how to deploy these apps to the cloud using **AWS** and **Azure**.

In the next chapter, we will explore **cloud deployment** in more detail, covering strategies for scaling and maintaining your applications in a production environment.

Let's continue building!

Chapter 9

Microservices and Event-Driven Architecture

In this chapter, we will dive deep into **microservices** and **event-driven architecture**, exploring why they are critical for building **scalable, maintainable**, and **resilient systems**. We will discuss how **Python** and **C#** fit into these architectures, and look at tools like **RabbitMQ, Kafka**, and **Azure Service Bus** for implementing **event-driven services**. Lastly, we will walk through a **real-world case study** on **breaking a monolithic application into microservices**.

9.1 Why Microservices? How Python & C# Fit into Scalable Systems

1. Introduction to Microservices

Microservices architecture is an approach to designing applications as a collection of loosely coupled, independently deployable services. Each microservice is focused on a specific business capability, allowing teams to work on different services independently while maintaining a clear separation of concerns.

- **Key Characteristics**:
    - o **Decentralized data management**: Each microservice manages its own database or data source.
    - o **Independent deployment**: Each service can be deployed and scaled independently.
    - o **Resilience and fault isolation**: If one microservice fails, the others continue to function.
    - o **Technology-agnostic**: Each microservice can be developed using the best-suited technology stack (e.g., **Python** or **C#**).

2. Why Microservices?

- **Scalability**: Microservices allow for fine-grained **scaling** of individual services based on demand. For example, if the **payment service** of your e-commerce application needs more resources, it can be scaled without affecting other parts of the system.

- **Agility**: Teams can work on different services independently, leading to faster development cycles and better flexibility in choosing the technology that fits the problem.

- **Fault Isolation**: Microservices provide better **resilience** since each service is isolated. Failure in one service doesn't cause the entire system to fail.

- **Easier Maintenance**: Microservices, due to their small, independent nature, are easier to understand and maintain.

3. How Python and C# Fit into Microservices

- **Python in Microservices**:
  - **Flexibility**: Python's simplicity makes it an excellent choice for building small, lightweight microservices.
  - **Popular Frameworks**: Frameworks like **FastAPI**, **Flask**, and **Django REST Framework** allow Python developers to quickly build scalable APIs and microservices.
  - **Data Processing and Machine Learning**: Python is ideal for services that involve **data processing**, **machine learning**, and **AI**.

- **C# in Microservices**:

- o **Performance and Scalability**: **ASP.NET Core** is a high-performance framework ideal for building microservices.
- o **Integration with Azure**: C# works seamlessly with **Azure**, which is a preferred cloud platform for many enterprises.
- o **Robust Ecosystem**: **.NET Core** provides strong support for building microservices with **Docker**, **Kubernetes**, and **CI/CD pipelines** for easy deployment and scaling.

9.2 Implementing Event-Driven Services using RabbitMQ, Kafka, and Azure Service Bus

Event-driven architecture is a pattern where **events** trigger actions or processes. In microservices, **asynchronous communication** via events helps to decouple services, allowing them to interact without needing direct API calls.

1. Event-Driven Architecture Overview

- **Event Producers**: Services that emit events (e.g., **Order Service, Payment Service**).
- **Event Consumers**: Services that listen for and react to events (e.g., **Notification Service, Inventory Service**).
- **Event Broker**: The intermediary (e.g., **RabbitMQ, Kafka, Azure Service Bus**) that delivers events to consumers.

2. RabbitMQ

RabbitMQ is an open-source message broker that facilitates communication between services by sending and receiving **messages** in a queue-based system.

- **Advantages**:
  - Supports **reliable message delivery** and **asynchronous communication**.
  - Widely adopted for **task queuing** and **event-driven microservices**.
- **Example**:
  - Install **RabbitMQ**:

bash

```
sudo apt-get install rabbitmq-server
```

o Python with **pika** (RabbitMQ library):

```python
python

import pika

connection                              =
pika.BlockingConnection(pika.Connec
tionParameters('localhost'))
channel = connection.channel()

# Declare a queue
channel.queue_declare(queue='task_q
ueue')

# Sending a message
channel.basic_publish(exchange='',
routing_key='task_queue', body='Task
message')

print(" [x] Sent 'Task message'")
connection.close()
```

3. Kafka

Kafka is a distributed streaming platform for building **real-time event-driven systems**.

- **Advantages**:

125

- o Kafka excels at handling high-throughput, real-time event streams.
- o It supports **fault tolerance**, allowing events to be replicated across multiple nodes.
- o Useful for handling large-scale, **event-driven architectures**.

- **Example**:
  - o **Kafka producer** in Python using **confluent-kafka**:

```python
from confluent_kafka import Producer

def delivery_report(err, msg):
    if err is not None:
        print('Message        delivery
failed: {}'.format(err))
    else:
        print('Message delivered to
{}          [{}]'.format(msg.topic(),
msg.partition()))

p = Producer({'bootstrap.servers':
'localhost:9092'})
p.produce('my_topic',      key='key',
value='value',
callback=delivery_report)
p.flush()
```

4. Azure Service Bus

Azure Service Bus is a fully managed **message queuing** service provided by Microsoft, ideal for decoupling microservices and enabling reliable asynchronous messaging.

- **Advantages**:
  - ○ Fully managed and scalable messaging service that integrates well with **Azure**.
  - ○ Supports **queues**, **topics**, and **subscriptions**, allowing for advanced routing of messages.
- **Example**:
  - ○ **Sending a message to an Azure Service Bus Queue** using **C#**:

```csharp
var        connectionString        =
"your_connection_string";
var      queueClient      =      new
QueueClient(connectionString,
"myqueue");

var      message      =      new
Message(Encoding.UTF8.GetBytes("Hel
lo, Azure Service Bus!"));
```

127

```
await
queueClient.SendAsync(message);
```

9.3 Real-World Case Study: Breaking a Monolithic App into Microservices

In this section, we'll walk through a **real-world case study** of **breaking a monolithic application** into **microservices**. Let's assume we have a simple **e-commerce application** that handles everything in a single monolithic app, including user authentication, order management, payment processing, and inventory tracking.

1. Step 1: Identify Service Boundaries

The first step is to identify and **separate responsibilities** within the monolith. The main **services** in the e-commerce app could be:

- **User Service**: Manages user authentication and profiles.
- **Order Service**: Handles order creation and processing.
- **Payment Service**: Manages payments and transactions.
- **Inventory Service**: Tracks available stock and manages product listings.

128

Each of these services can be built as an independent microservice, with its own database and API.

2. Step 2: Decouple Services using Events

Next, we use an **event-driven architecture** to decouple these services. For example:

- When an order is created in the **Order Service**, it emits an event like `OrderCreated`.
- The **Inventory Service** listens for this event and updates the stock accordingly.
- The **Payment Service** subscribes to the event and processes the payment.

3. Step 3: Implement Event-Driven Communication

We can use **RabbitMQ** or **Kafka** to implement the messaging layer between services.

- **Order Service** emits an `OrderCreated` event.
- **Payment Service** listens for the `OrderCreated` event and starts the payment process.
- **Inventory Service** listens for the `OrderCreated` event and reserves the items.

This **asynchronous communication** allows services to operate independently without waiting for each other.

4. Step 4: Deploy Microservices

Once the services are implemented, deploy each service independently using **Docker** and **Kubernetes** for containerization and orchestration.

- **Docker** containers will encapsulate each microservice.
- **Kubernetes** will manage the scaling and networking of these containers.

5. Step 5: Monitor and Scale Services

Finally, we can **monitor** and **scale** each service based on its load using tools like **Prometheus** and **Grafana** for monitoring, and **Kubernetes**'s horizontal scaling capabilities to handle increased traffic for individual services.

Conclusion

In this chapter, we explored the power of **microservices** and **event-driven architecture** in building **scalable** and **resilient systems**. We discussed how **Python** and **C#** fit into these architectures, focusing on tools like **RabbitMQ**, **Kafka**, and **Azure Service Bus** for implementing event-driven communication. The **real-world case study** provided a clear example of how to **break a monolithic app** into microservices and scale them independently.

In the next chapter, we'll dive into **advanced topics** like **service discovery**, **API gateways**, and **distributed tracing** in microservice architectures.

Let's continue scaling!

Chapter 10

Serverless Computing with Python and C#

Serverless computing has revolutionized the way we build and deploy applications by allowing developers to focus on business logic without worrying about the underlying infrastructure. In this chapter, we will explore **serverless computing** and demonstrate how to build **serverless applications** using **Python** and **C#**. We will also walk through a **real-world case study** of creating an **auto-scaling email service** using **AWS Lambda**, **Azure Functions**, and **Google Cloud Functions**.

10.1 Introduction to AWS Lambda, Azure Functions, and Google Cloud Functions

1. What is Serverless Computing?

Serverless computing allows you to build and run applications without managing the **servers** or **infrastructure**. The cloud provider handles everything from **provisioning** and **scaling** to **monitoring** and **maintenance**.

- **Key Characteristics**:
  - **Event-driven**: Functions are triggered by events (e.g., HTTP requests, database updates, file uploads).
  - **Scalable**: Automatically scales based on the workload, meaning no need to worry about provisioning servers.
  - **Cost-effective**: You only pay for the resources you use, rather than paying for idle server time.

2. AWS Lambda

AWS Lambda is Amazon's **serverless compute service**. It allows you to run code in response to events like **HTTP requests, file uploads to S3**, and **changes in DynamoDB**.

- **Key Features**:
  - **Event-driven**: Trigger functions based on AWS events or external services.

133

- o **Automatic scaling**: Automatically scales based on traffic.
- o **Supports multiple languages**: Python, Node.js, Java, C#, Go, and more.
- o **Pay-as-you-go** pricing model: Charges based on the number of requests and execution time.

3. Azure Functions

Azure Functions is Microsoft's serverless compute offering. It allows you to run small pieces of code in response to various events, from HTTP requests to timer-based triggers.

- **Key Features**:
  - o **Event-driven**: Supports triggers from Azure services (e.g., Event Grid, Blob Storage, HTTP requests).
  - o **Integrated with Azure services**: Seamlessly integrates with **Azure Logic Apps, Cosmos DB**, and other Azure services.
  - o **Multiple language support**: C#, Python, JavaScript, and Java.
  - o **Scaling**: Automatically scales to handle requests.

4. Google Cloud Functions

Google Cloud Functions is Google's serverless compute platform that lets you run functions triggered by cloud events or HTTP requests.

- **Key Features**:
    - **Lightweight**: Build and deploy functions quickly without worrying about infrastructure.
    - **Integration with Google Cloud**: Easily integrates with **Firebase**, **Google Pub/Sub**, and **Cloud Storage**.
    - **Automatic scaling**: Functions scale dynamically based on incoming traffic.
    - **Multiple languages**: Python, Go, Node.js, Java, and more.

10.2 Writing Serverless Applications in Python and C#

Let's now explore how to write **serverless applications** in both **Python** and **C#**. We will use **AWS Lambda** and **Azure**

Functions as our platforms of choice to illustrate how to create, deploy, and manage serverless functions.

1. Python Example: AWS Lambda

To create a serverless function in **AWS Lambda** using Python, follow these steps:

1. **Create a Lambda function** in the AWS Management Console.
2. **Write the function** in Python:

```python
python

import json

def lambda_handler(event, context):
    name = event.get('name', 'World')
    return {
        'statusCode': 200,
        'body':        json.dumps(f'Hello,
{name}!')
    }
```

3. **Deploy the function**:
   - AWS will handle provisioning the infrastructure and scaling your function based on demand.

136

- o You can trigger this function via **API Gateway**, **S3**, or other AWS services.

4. **Invoke the function** via an HTTP request:

- o Using **API Gateway**, you can expose the function via an HTTP endpoint that clients can call.

2. C# Example: Azure Functions

For **C#** and **Azure Functions**, we will create a simple HTTP-triggered function.

1. **Create an Azure Function** in the Azure portal.
2. **Write the function** in C#:

```csharp
using Microsoft.AspNetCore.Http;
using Microsoft.Extensions.Logging;
using System.IO;
using System.Threading.Tasks;

public static class HelloFunction
{
    [FunctionName("HelloFunction")]
    public static async Task RunAsync(

[HttpTrigger(AuthorizationLevel.Function,
"get", "post")] HttpRequest req,
```

```
        ILogger log)
    {
        string name = req.Query["name"];
        if (string.IsNullOrEmpty(name))
        {
            name = "World";
        }
        log.LogInformation($"Saying  hello
to {name}");
        await
req.HttpContext.Response.WriteAsync($"Hel
lo, {name}!");
    }
}
```

3. **Deploy the function** to Azure.
   - o Azure automatically handles scaling the function in response to incoming HTTP requests.

4. **Invoke the function** via an HTTP request:
   - o You can test this function by sending a GET or POST request to the function's endpoint.

3. Google Cloud Functions (Python)

Here's an example of a Google Cloud Function using Python:

1. **Write the function** in Python:

138

```python
python

def hello_world(request):
    return "Hello, World!"
```

2. **Deploy the function** using the Google Cloud CLI:

```bash
bash

gcloud functions deploy hello_world --
runtime python310 --trigger-http
```

3. **Invoke the function** via an HTTP request:

   o You'll get a URL that you can use to make HTTP requests to invoke your function.

10.3 Case Study: Creating an Auto-Scaling Email Service

In this case study, we will build a simple **auto-scaling email service** using serverless computing. The email service will receive an HTTP request with the recipient's email and message content, and send an email asynchronously.

139

1. Problem Definition

We need a service that:

- Accepts HTTP requests with email data (recipient, message, etc.).
- Sends the email using an external email API (e.g., **SendGrid, Amazon SES**).
- Scales automatically based on traffic.

2. Architecture Overview

- **API Gateway** (AWS) or **Azure API Management** will handle incoming HTTP requests.
- **AWS Lambda** or **Azure Functions** will process the requests asynchronously.
- The function will interact with an **email service provider** like **SendGrid** or **Amazon SES** to send the emails.

3. Implementation in Python (AWS Lambda)

- **Create a Lambda function** to handle email requests.
- Use the **SendGrid** API to send emails.

Example Lambda function:

```python
```

```python
import json
import sendgrid
from sendgrid.helpers.mail import Mail, Email,
To, Content

def lambda_handler(event, context):
    recipient_email = event['email']
    message_body = event['message']

    sg                               =
sendgrid.SendGridAPIClient(api_key='your_sendgr
id_api_key')
    from_email            =            Email("no-
reply@yourdomain.com")
    to_email = To(recipient_email)
    content         =          Content("text/plain",
message_body)
    mail = Mail(from_email, to_email, "Subject:
Test Email", content)

    try:
        response                              =
sg.client.mail.send.post(request_body=mail.get(
))
        return {
            'statusCode': 200,
            'body':     json.dumps('Email     sent
successfully')
        }
```

```
except Exception as e:
    return {
        'statusCode': 500,
        'body':          json.dumps(f"Error:
{str(e)}")
    }
```

4. Deploying the Service

1. **Deploy the Lambda function** using AWS.

2. **Set up an API Gateway** to trigger the Lambda function.

3. The service will **auto-scale** to handle large numbers of email requests.

5. Auto-Scaling Considerations

- **AWS Lambda** automatically scales based on the number of requests.

- **Email API providers** (like **SendGrid**) also provide automatic scaling, ensuring the service can handle large email volumes without needing manual intervention.

Conclusion

In this chapter, we explored **serverless computing** and demonstrated how to build serverless applications using

AWS Lambda, **Azure Functions**, and **Google Cloud Functions** with **Python** and **C#**. We also worked through a **real-world case study** of creating an **auto-scaling email service**, highlighting the benefits of serverless architecture in handling variable workloads with ease.

In the next chapter, we will continue building on this knowledge to explore **monitoring and logging** in serverless applications, ensuring they are efficient and scalable in a production environment.

Let's continue building! 🚀

Chapter 11

AI and Machine Learning for Developers

In this chapter, we will explore how **AI** and **machine learning (ML)** can be integrated into **Python** and **C#** applications. We'll discuss how to leverage powerful **AI models** and **cloud-based AI tools** to build intelligent systems. We'll also guide you through a **hands-on project** where we will build an **AI-powered chatbot**. Additionally, we will look at popular **cloud-based AI services** like **Azure AI**, **OpenAI**, and **Google Vertex AI**.

11.1 Integrating AI Models into Python and C# Applications

Integrating AI models into your applications can significantly enhance their functionality, enabling them to perform tasks like **speech recognition**, **image**

144

classification, **text analysis**, and more. Let's explore how to integrate AI into both **Python** and **C#**.

1. AI in Python

Python has become the go-to language for AI and machine learning, thanks to its **rich ecosystem** of libraries and frameworks.

- **Popular Libraries for AI/ML**:
    - **TensorFlow**: Open-source framework for machine learning.
    - **PyTorch**: Another popular framework for deep learning and neural networks.
    - **Scikit-learn**: Ideal for traditional machine learning algorithms (e.g., regression, classification).
    - **NLTK**: Natural Language Toolkit for text processing.
    - **spaCy**: A library for advanced natural language processing.
- **Example: Integrating a Pretrained AI Model in Python** Here's how you might use a **pretrained sentiment analysis model** from **Hugging Face** in Python:

```python
python

from transformers import pipeline

# Load a pretrained model for sentiment
analysis
sentiment_analyzer = pipeline('sentiment-
analysis')

# Use the model to analyze the sentiment of
a text
result = sentiment_analyzer("I love this
product!")
print(result)
```

This example leverages the **Hugging Face** library, which provides easy access to pretrained models, making it simple to integrate AI features into your Python applications.

2. AI in C#

While Python is the dominant language in the AI field, **C#** can also be used effectively for integrating AI into applications, particularly when building **enterprise-level systems** with the **Microsoft ecosystem**.

- **Popular Libraries for AI/ML in C#**:

146

- ○ **ML.NET**: A Microsoft framework for machine learning in C# that supports **training models** and **integrating them into .NET applications**.
- ○ **Accord.NET**: A framework for scientific computing that includes AI and machine learning algorithms.
- ○ **TensorFlow.NET**: A .NET binding to the TensorFlow machine learning framework.

- **Example: Using ML.NET for Classification**
  Here's a simple example of using **ML.NET** to perform a **binary classification** task in C#:

```csharp
using Microsoft.ML;
using Microsoft.ML.Data;
using System;

public class SentimentData
{
    public string Text { get; set; }
    public bool Label { get; set; }
}

public class SentimentPrediction :
SentimentData
{
    public float Prediction { get; set; }
```

147

```
}

class Program
{
    static void Main(string[] args)
    {
        var context = new MLContext();

        var data = new[] {
            new SentimentData { Text = "I
love this product!", Label = true },
            new SentimentData { Text =
"This is terrible.", Label = false }
        };

        var trainData =
context.Data.LoadFromEnumerable(data);

        var pipeline =
context.Transforms.Text.FeaturizeText("Fe
atures", "Text")

.Append(context.BinaryClassification.Trai
ners.SdcaLogisticRegression("Label",
"Features"));

        var model =
pipeline.Fit(trainData);
```

```
        var        predictionFunction        =
model.CreatePredictionFunction<SentimentD
ata, SentimentPrediction>(context);

        var           prediction         =
predictionFunction.Predict(new
SentimentData { Text = "This is amazing!"
});
        Console.WriteLine($"Prediction:
{prediction.Prediction}");
    }
}
```

In this example, we use **ML.NET** to create a machine learning model that predicts the sentiment of text input.

11.2 Hands-On Project: Building an AI-Powered Chatbot

Now let's build an **AI-powered chatbot** using **Python** and **C#**. The chatbot will be able to respond to simple user inputs using a **pretrained AI model** for **natural language processing (NLP)**.

149

1. Python Chatbot with Hugging Face

To build an AI-powered chatbot in Python, we'll use **Hugging Face's transformer models**, which are great for **language understanding** and **text generation**.

- **Install Hugging Face and Dependencies**:

bash

```
pip install transformers torch
```

- **Chatbot Code**:

python

```
from transformers import pipeline

# Initialize the chatbot with a pre-trained
conversational model
chatbot    =    pipeline("conversational",
model="microsoft/DialoGPT-medium")

while True:
    user_input = input("You: ")
    if user_input.lower() == "exit":
        print("Goodbye!")
        break
```

```
# Get the chatbot response
response = chatbot(user_input)
print(f"Bot:
{response[0]['generated_text']}")
```

This simple chatbot uses a **DialoGPT** model, a conversational model built by **Microsoft** that can hold short conversations. The chatbot will continue responding to the user until "exit" is typed.

2. C# Chatbot with ML.NET and Text Classification

In C#, we can create a **simple rule-based chatbot** or use **ML.NET** for more complex text classification.

- **Setting Up a Simple Rule-Based Chatbot**:

```csharp
csharp

using System;

class Program
{
    static void Main()
    {
        Console.WriteLine("Bot: Hello, how can I assist you today?");
        while (true)
        {
```

```
        string      userInput     =
Console.ReadLine();
        if
(userInput.ToLower().Contains("hello"))
            {
                Console.WriteLine("Bot:
Hi! How can I help?");
            }
        else                        if
(userInput.ToLower().Contains("bye"))
            {
                Console.WriteLine("Bot:
Goodbye!");
                break;
            }
        else
            {
                Console.WriteLine("Bot:  I
didn't understand that.");
            }
        }
    }
}
```

This **simple rule-based** chatbot looks for keywords like "hello" and "bye" to determine the response. It's a basic implementation, but you can extend it by integrating **ML.NET** or external services like

Dialogflow or **Microsoft Bot Framework** for more intelligent responses.

11.3 Cloud-Based AI Tools: Azure AI, OpenAI, Google Vertex AI

In addition to local models, cloud-based AI services offer advanced features like **scalable training**, **real-time inference**, and integration with other cloud services. Let's explore some of the leading cloud-based AI tools.

1. Azure AI

Azure AI offers a broad set of tools and services for building AI-powered applications, including **vision**, **speech**, and **language processing**.

- **Azure Cognitive Services** includes APIs for **text analysis**, **speech recognition**, and **image recognition**.
- You can deploy models using **Azure Machine Learning**, which provides end-to-end workflows for building, training, and deploying models at scale.

153

Example: Using Azure Cognitive Services for Text Analysis in C#:

```csharp
using
Microsoft.Azure.CognitiveServices.Language.Text
Analytics;
using
Microsoft.Azure.CognitiveServices.Language.Text
Analytics.Models;
using Microsoft.Rest.Azure.Authentication;

var              credentials              =
ApplicationTokenProvider.LoginWithServicePrinci
palSecret("your-client-id",     "your-secret",
"your-tenant-id");
var         client         =         new
TextAnalyticsClient(credentials)
{
    Endpoint        =          "https://your-
endpoint.cognitiveservices.azure.com/"
};

var result = await client.SentimentAsync(false,
new MultiLanguageBatchInput(
    new List<MultiLanguageInput>
    {
```

```
        new   MultiLanguageInput("en",   "1",   "I
love programming!")
    }));
```

```
Console.WriteLine(result.Documents[0].Sentiment
);
```

OpenAI provides some of the most advanced models for natural language processing and generation, including **GPT-3**, which powers a variety of intelligent systems.

- **GPT-3** enables highly **dynamic conversations** and **content generation** and can be used to integrate complex conversational models into chatbots and customer service applications.
- **Example**: Using **GPT-3** in Python via the **OpenAI API**:

```python
import openai

openai.api_key = 'your-api-key'

response = openai.Completion.create(
    engine="text-davinci-003",
    prompt="What's the weather like today?",
```

```
      max_tokens=50
)
```

```
print(response.choices[0].text.strip())
```

3. Google Vertex AI

Google Vertex AI provides a comprehensive platform for building, training, and deploying AI models with **machine learning workflows**. It integrates seamlessly with **Google Cloud Storage**, **BigQuery**, and **AutoML** to simplify the process.

- Vertex AI helps developers with everything from **data preprocessing** to **model deployment**, making it easier to integrate ML capabilities into production systems.

Example: Use **Google Cloud's AI tools** for **image classification** or **text analysis** within the Vertex AI platform.

Conclusion

In this chapter, we introduced how to integrate **AI and machine learning** into **Python** and **C#** applications. We built an **AI-powered chatbot** in both languages and explored the use of powerful **cloud-based AI tools** such as **Azure AI**, **OpenAI**, and **Google Vertex AI**. These services make it easier than ever to create intelligent systems that enhance the functionality of your applications.

In the next chapter, we will continue building by exploring **advanced cloud deployment strategies**, ensuring that your AI-powered systems scale seamlessly in production.

Let's continue building! 🚀

Chapter 12

Cloud-Native Application Development

In this chapter, we will explore the core principles of **cloud-native application development**, which emphasizes building applications that are optimized for **cloud environments**. We will cover how to deploy applications on major cloud platforms like **Azure**, **AWS**, and **Google Cloud**, and how to leverage **Docker** and **Kubernetes** for containerized deployments. We'll also walk through a **real-world case study** of **scaling a SaaS app with Kubernetes**.

12.1 Deploying Applications on Azure, AWS, and Google Cloud

Deploying cloud-native applications requires an understanding of the deployment services provided by each cloud provider. Let's explore how to deploy applications on

Azure, **AWS**, and **Google Cloud**, focusing on the managed services they offer for cloud-native applications.

1. Deploying on Azure

Azure provides a suite of services to support cloud-native development, including **Azure App Services**, **Azure Kubernetes Service (AKS)**, and **Azure Functions** for serverless computing.

- **Azure App Services**:
  - A fully managed platform for building and hosting web applications.
  - Supports **.NET**, **Node.js**, **Java**, **Python**, and other frameworks.
  - Handles **scaling, patching**, and **maintenance** for you.

  Example: Deploying a Python app on **Azure App Service**:

4. **Create an Azure App Service** using the **Azure Portal**.
    5. **Publish your code** from **Visual Studio** or **VS Code** to the App Service.
    6. Azure handles **scaling** based on incoming traffic.
- **Azure Kubernetes Service (AKS)**:

- A fully managed **Kubernetes** service that simplifies the deployment and management of containerized applications.
- AKS automates the process of deploying, managing, and scaling containerized applications.

Example: Deploying a containerized app on **AKS**:

2. **Build a Docker image** for your application.
3. Push the image to **Azure Container Registry**.
4. Create a Kubernetes **deployment** and **service** on AKS.

2. Deploying on AWS

AWS provides various services for deploying cloud-native applications, including **Elastic Beanstalk, Amazon ECS, and Amazon EKS** (Elastic Kubernetes Service).

- **Elastic Beanstalk**:
  - A platform-as-a-service (PaaS) that supports **Java, .NET, Node.js, Python**, and more.
  - Elastic Beanstalk automatically handles the **deployment, scaling**, and **monitoring**.

160

Example: Deploying a Node.js app on **Elastic Beanstalk**:

3.   **Package your app** as a ZIP file.

   4.   **Deploy to Elastic Beanstalk** using the AWS Management Console or the **AWS CLI**.

- **Amazon ECS and EKS**:

   o   **Amazon ECS** is a fully managed container orchestration service for Docker containers.

   o   **Amazon EKS** is a managed Kubernetes service that simplifies running Kubernetes on AWS.

Example: Deploying a Docker container on **ECS**:

   2.   **Build your Docker image**.

   3.   Push the image to **Amazon ECR** (Elastic Container Registry).

   4.   Create a **task definition** and run it in ECS.

3. Deploying on Google Cloud

Google Cloud offers services like **Google App Engine**, **Google Kubernetes Engine (GKE)**, and **Cloud Functions** for building and deploying cloud-native apps.

- **Google App Engine**:

- o A fully managed serverless platform that supports multiple programming languages.
- o Automatically scales your app based on traffic.

Example: Deploying a Python app on **App Engine**:

3. **Create a Python app**.

   4. Deploy using the **Google Cloud SDK**:

```bash
bash

gcloud app deploy
```

- **Google Kubernetes Engine (GKE)**:
  - o A fully managed Kubernetes service for running containerized applications.
  - o GKE handles the **provisioning, scaling**, and **management** of Kubernetes clusters.

Example: Deploying a Docker container on **GKE**:

2. **Build and push** your Docker image to **Google Container Registry**.
3. Create a **deployment** and **service** using Kubernetes YAML files.

12.2 Using Docker & Kubernetes for Containerized Deployments

Containerization is a core aspect of **cloud-native development** because it allows developers to **package applications and their dependencies** in a way that makes them **portable, scalable**, and **resilient**.

1. Docker

Docker is an open-source platform for automating the deployment of applications in **containers**. Containers are lightweight, portable, and ensure that the app runs the same way across any environment (development, testing, production).

- **Key Features**:
    - **Isolation**: Containers provide isolated environments, ensuring that dependencies don't conflict.
    - **Portability**: Docker containers can run on any system that supports Docker, from a developer's laptop to production systems in the cloud.

- o **Versioning**: Docker allows for versioning of containers, making it easier to roll back to previous versions.

- **Dockerfile**:
  - o A **Dockerfile** is a script that contains a set of instructions to build a Docker image.

Example: Dockerfile for a Python app:

```
dockerfile

FROM python:3.8-slim

WORKDIR /app
  . /app

RUN pip install -r requirements.txt

CMD ["python", "app.py"]
```

- **Building and Running a Docker Container**:
1. **Build the Docker image**:

```
bash

docker build -t myapp .
```

2. **Run the Docker container**:

164

```bash
docker run -p 5000:5000 myapp
```

2. Kubernetes

Kubernetes is a powerful platform for managing containerized applications at scale. It automates the deployment, scaling, and operations of application containers.

- **Key Concepts**:
  - **Pods**: The smallest deployable units in Kubernetes, typically running one container.
  - **Deployments**: Manage stateless applications and can automatically scale the number of pods.
  - **Services**: Expose your application to other services or the external world.
  - **ConfigMaps and Secrets**: Store and manage configuration settings and sensitive information.
- **Setting Up Kubernetes Cluster**: You can use **Google Kubernetes Engine (GKE)**, **AWS EKS**, or **Azure AKS** to set up a managed Kubernetes cluster. Here's how you would deploy an app to Kubernetes:
1. **Create a Deployment YAML file**:

```yaml
```

```
apiVersion: apps/v1
kind: Deployment
metadata:
  name: myapp
spec:
  replicas: 3
  selector:
    matchLabels:
      app: myapp
  template:
    metadata:
      labels:
        app: myapp
    spec:
      containers:
      - name: myapp
        image: myapp:v1
        ports:
        - containerPort: 5000
```

2.   **Apply the Deployment**:

```bash
bash
```

```
kubectl apply -f deployment.yaml
```

3.   **Expose the Application**: Create a **Service** to expose the app externally:

```yaml
yaml

apiVersion: v1
kind: Service
metadata:
  name: myapp-service
spec:
  selector:
    app: myapp
  ports:
    - protocol: TCP
      port: 80
      targetPort: 5000
  type: LoadBalancer
```

4.   **Scale the Application**: Kubernetes can scale your application based on demand:

```bash
bash

kubectl scale deployment myapp --
replicas=5
```

12.3 Case Study: Scaling a SaaS App with Kubernetes

In this case study, we will walk through how to **scale a SaaS app** using **Kubernetes**. Let's assume we have a **SaaS application** built with **Python (Flask)** or **C# (ASP.NET Core)**. This app is initially deployed with one container running on **AWS EKS** (Elastic Kubernetes Service).

1. Scaling Challenge

Our SaaS application is receiving increased traffic, and we need to **scale the app horizontally** by adding more instances of the service without compromising performance. Kubernetes is the perfect tool for this scenario because it allows us to scale automatically based on traffic.

2. Deploying the App to Kubernetes

We begin by **containerizing** the app and deploying it to a Kubernetes cluster on **AWS EKS**.

- **Create Docker Images** for the Python or C# app.
- **Push the Docker images** to **Amazon ECR** (Elastic Container Registry).
- Create a **Kubernetes Deployment** to manage scaling.

3. Auto-Scaling with Kubernetes

Kubernetes makes it easy to **automatically scale** the app based on CPU or memory usage. For example:

- **Horizontal Pod Autoscaling** (HPA) automatically scales the number of pod replicas based on the **CPU usage** or **memory usage**.

HPA Example:

```bash
bash
```

```
kubectl   autoscale   deployment   myapp   --cpu-
percent=50 --min=2 --max=10
```

This command sets up an **autoscaler** that will keep the CPU usage at or below 50%, scaling between 2 and 10 replicas.

4. Load Balancing and High Availability

Kubernetes ensures **high availability** by distributing pods across different nodes and using **load balancing** to distribute incoming traffic evenly across multiple instances of the app.

5. Continuous Monitoring and Logging

We can use **Prometheus** and **Grafana** for **monitoring**, and **Elasticsearch** and **Kibana** for **logging** to ensure that the app is running smoothly and scaling as needed.

Conclusion

In this chapter, we explored **cloud-native application development**, focusing on deploying applications to **Azure, AWS**, and **Google Cloud**. We also covered how to use **Docker** and **Kubernetes** to containerize and scale applications. Finally, we looked at a **real-world case study** of **scaling a SaaS app with Kubernetes**, demonstrating the power of Kubernetes for managing scalable, resilient cloud-native applications.

In the next chapter, we will focus on **cloud security** best practices for securing cloud-native applications and their deployments.

Let's continue building! 🚀

Part 5

Cross-Platform Mobile and Game Development

Chapter 13

Mobile App Development with Python (Kivy) and C# (.NET MAUI, Xamarin)

In this chapter, we will dive into **cross-platform mobile development**, focusing on popular frameworks like **Kivy** for Python and **.NET MAUI** and **Xamarin** for C#. Cross-platform frameworks allow developers to write applications once and deploy them on both **iOS** and **Android** without needing to rewrite the code for each platform. We will also walk through a **hands-on project** where we build a **simple finance tracker app** and discuss debugging and performance optimization techniques.

13.1 Introduction to Cross-Platform Mobile Frameworks

Cross-platform mobile frameworks are designed to help developers build applications that can run on **multiple platforms** (iOS, Android) using a single codebase. Let's

172

explore the most widely used frameworks for **Python** and **C#**.

1. Kivy (Python)

Kivy is a **Python framework** that allows you to develop **cross-platform applications**, including **mobile apps**. It supports **Android, iOS, Linux, Windows**, and **macOS**.

- **Key Features**:
    - Open-source and free to use.
    - **Multi-touch support** and designed for **touch-based** applications.
    - Works well for **mobile apps, games**, and **interactive applications**.
    - Provides a **rich set of widgets** for creating UIs.
- **Best Use Cases**:
    - Ideal for creating apps that need to run on **multiple platforms** without heavy reliance on platform-specific features.
    - Great for applications with **touch-based UIs**.

2. .NET MAUI (C#)

.NET MAUI (Multi-platform App UI) is a **cross-platform framework** for building **native mobile apps** with **C#**. It's the successor to **Xamarin** and provides a unified framework for building apps for **Android, iOS, macOS**, and **Windows**.

- **Key Features**:
  - o **Single codebase** for mobile and desktop apps.
  - o **Native controls** and access to platform-specific APIs.
  - o Seamless integration with **XAML** for UI design and **C#** for business logic.
  - o **Community and enterprise support** from Microsoft.
- **Best Use Cases**:
  - o Ideal for developers working in the **Microsoft ecosystem**.
  - o Great for apps that need to run on both **mobile and desktop** platforms.

3. Xamarin (C#)

Xamarin is a cross-platform mobile framework that allows developers to write applications for **iOS, Android**, and **Windows** using **C#** and **.NET**. Xamarin uses a single **C# codebase** to build native applications for all three platforms.

- **Key Features**:

- o **Full access** to native APIs and controls on iOS and Android.
- o Allows **native performance** and access to platform-specific features.
- o **Xamarin.Forms** allows you to create **UI code** shared across platforms.

- **Best Use Cases**:
  - o Ideal for **C# developers** who want to build native applications with access to platform-specific features.
  - o Suitable for teams that are already invested in the **.NET ecosystem**.

13.2 Hands-On Project: Building a Simple Finance Tracker for iOS & Android

Now, let's walk through building a **simple finance tracker app** using both **Kivy** (Python) and **.NET MAUI** (C#). This app will allow users to track their expenses and incomes, displaying them in a simple interface. We'll cover the basic app structure, UI components, and how to deploy the app on **iOS** and **Android**.

1. Building the Finance Tracker App with Kivy (Python)

Let's start by creating a basic finance tracker app using **Kivy**. We'll implement a simple **UI** to input **expenses** and **incomes**, and display them in a list.

- **Install Kivy**: First, install **Kivy** and the dependencies:

bash

```
pip install kivy
```

- **Basic App Structure**: The app will have the following components:
    - **Text input** for entering the amount and description of each transaction.
    - **ListView** for displaying transactions.
    - **Button** to add the transaction to the list.

Here's the code for the app:

python

```
from kivy.app import App
```

```python
from kivy.uix.boxlayout import BoxLayout
from kivy.uix.textinput import TextInput
from kivy.uix.button import Button
from kivy.uix.label import Label
from kivy.uix.scrollview import ScrollView

class FinanceApp(App):
    def build(self):
        self.transactions = []
        self.main_layout                    =
BoxLayout(orientation='vertical')

        self.amount_input                   =
TextInput(hint_text='Enter amount')
        self.description_input              =
TextInput(hint_text='Enter description')
        self.add_button = Button(text='Add
Transaction')

self.add_button.bind(on_press=self.add_tr
ansaction)


self.main_layout.add_widget(self.amount_i
nput)


self.main_layout.add_widget(self.descript
ion_input)
```

```
self.main_layout.add_widget(self.add_butt
on)

        self.transaction_list           =
ScrollView()
        self.transactions_layout         =
BoxLayout(orientation='vertical',
size_hint_y=None)

self.transactions_layout.bind(minimum_hei
ght=self.transactions_layout.setter('heig
ht'))

self.transaction_list.add_widget(self.tra
nsactions_layout)


self.main_layout.add_widget(self.transact
ion_list)

        return self.main_layout

    def add_transaction(self, instance):
        amount = self.amount_input.text
        description                      =
self.description_input.text
        if amount and description:
```

```
            transaction = f"{description}:
{amount}"
            label                    =
Label(text=transaction,  size_hint_y=None,
height=40)

self.transactions_layout.add_widget(label
)
            self.amount_input.text = ''
            self.description_input.text  =
''


if __name__ == '__main__':
    FinanceApp().run()
```

- **Running the App**: You can run this app on **Android** using **Buildozer** (for Android) or **Xcode** (for iOS), but the Kivy framework provides great flexibility for building cross-platform applications.

2. Building the Finance Tracker App with .NET MAUI (C#)

Now, let's build the same app using **.NET MAUI** for **cross-platform** mobile development.

- **Install .NET MAUI**: First, ensure you have the **.NET 6 SDK** installed on your system. Follow the installation instructions on the official Microsoft site.

179

- **Basic App Structure**: Create a new .NET MAUI app:

bash

```bash
dotnet new maui -n FinanceTracker
cd FinanceTracker
```

- **UI Layout and Code**: In **MainPage.xaml**, define the layout for your finance tracker app:

xml

```xml
<ContentPage
xmlns="http://schemas.microsoft.com/dotne
t/2021/maui"

xmlns:x="http://schemas.microsoft.com/win
fx/2006/xaml"

x:Class="FinanceTracker.MainPage">

    <StackLayout Padding="20">
        <Entry        x:Name="AmountEntry"
Placeholder="Enter              amount"
Keyboard="Numeric"/>
        <Entry   x:Name="DescriptionEntry"
Placeholder="Enter description"/>
```

```
        <Button    Text="Add    Transaction"
Clicked="OnAddTransactionClicked"/>
        <ListView
x:Name="TransactionListView">
            <ListView.ItemTemplate>
                <DataTemplate>
                    <TextCell
Text="{Binding          Description}"
Detail="{Binding Amount}"/>
                </DataTemplate>
            </ListView.ItemTemplate>
        </ListView>
    </StackLayout>

</ContentPage>
```

In **MainPage.xaml.cs**, add the logic for adding transactions:

csharp

```csharp
using Microsoft.Maui.Controls;
using System.Collections.ObjectModel;

namespace FinanceTracker
{
    public partial class MainPage : ContentPage
    {
```

181

```csharp
        ObservableCollection<Transaction>
transactions              =            new
ObservableCollection<Transaction>();

        public MainPage()
        {
            InitializeComponent();

TransactionListView.ItemsSource            =
transactions;
        }

        private                          void
OnAddTransactionClicked(object       sender,
EventArgs e)
        {
            string        amount          =
AmountEntry.Text;
            string     description        =
DescriptionEntry.Text;

            if
(!string.IsNullOrEmpty(amount)              &&
!string.IsNullOrEmpty(description))
            {
                transactions.Add(new
Transaction { Amount = amount, Description
= description });
```

```
                AmountEntry.Text        =
string.Empty;
                DescriptionEntry.Text   =
string.Empty;
            }
        }
    }

    public class Transaction
    {
        public string Amount { get; set; }
        public string Description { get;
set; }
    }
}
```

- **Running the App**: You can deploy this app on **Android** and **iOS** using **Visual Studio** or **Xcode**.

13.3 Debugging and Performance Optimization

Both **Python** and **C#** have robust tools for debugging and optimizing mobile apps.

1. Debugging in Python (Kivy)

- **Use Print Statements**: Print debugging is the easiest and quickest way to understand your app's behavior.
- **Use Logging**: The `logging` module in Python provides better control over output verbosity, helpful in production environments.

```python
python

import logging

logging.basicConfig(level=logging.DEBUG)
logging.debug("This is a debug message")
```

- **Use Android Studio** for debugging Android apps built with Kivy. It provides detailed logs and **debugging tools** for Android-specific issues.

2. Debugging in C# (.NET MAUI)

- **Visual Studio Debugger**: Visual Studio offers a powerful **debugger** with breakpoints, live variable inspection, and stepping through code.
- **Xamarin Inspector**: For **Xamarin** and **.NET MAUI** apps, the **Xamarin Inspector** allows you to run your app in a **debug mode** on iOS/Android and inspect the UI.

3. Performance Optimization

- **In Python**:
  - o Use **memory profiling tools** like **memory_profiler** to identify memory bottlenecks.
  - o Optimize **UI rendering** by minimizing the use of **heavy widgets** like `GridLayout` and opting for **simpler layouts** when possible.
- **In C#**:
  - o Use **Xamarin Profiler** and **Visual Studio Profiler** to identify performance issues in memory, CPU, and network usage.
  - o Use **async/await** to handle asynchronous tasks efficiently, preventing UI blocking.
  - o Use **native rendering** for better performance, as Xamarin allows integration with platform-specific native code.

Conclusion

In this chapter, we explored **cross-platform mobile development** with **Kivy** (Python) and **.NET MAUI** (C#).

We built a **simple finance tracker app** and discussed how to deploy it on **iOS** and **Android**. We also covered **debugging techniques** and **performance optimization** for both Python and C# applications, providing you with the necessary tools to create efficient and scalable mobile apps.

In the next chapter, we will focus on **game development** and how to build cross-platform games using **Unity** with **C#**, integrating real-time multiplayer features.

Let's continue building! 🚀

Chapter 14

Game Development with Python and C#

Game development is one of the most exciting and creative areas for developers, and with the rise of **cross-platform game engines**, building games that run on multiple devices has never been easier. In this chapter, we will explore two powerful game development tools: **Unity (C#)** and **Pygame (Python)**. We will compare the strengths of both platforms, look at how to build **2D** and **3D games** with them, and dive into a **real-world example** by creating a **multiplayer game prototype**.

14.1 Using Unity (C#) vs. Pygame (Python)

When it comes to building games, choosing the right framework can make a huge difference in the game's performance, ease of development, and platform compatibility. Let's break down **Unity** and **Pygame**, comparing them in terms of their features, use cases, and benefits for both **2D** and **3D** game development.

1. Unity (C#)

Unity is a **powerful game engine** used by professional game developers for creating both **2D and 3D games**. It's known for its versatility, robust community, and ability to export to multiple platforms (including **iOS**, **Android**, **PC**, **Consoles**, and **VR**).

- **Key Features**:
  - **Cross-platform support**: Unity supports over 25 platforms, including desktop, mobile, consoles, and VR/AR.
  - **3D and 2D game development**: Unity allows you to create both 2D and 3D games with high-quality rendering.
  - **Asset Store**: Unity has a massive asset store with ready-to-use models, textures, animations, and scripts.
  - **C# scripting**: Unity uses **C#** as its primary scripting language, which is widely recognized for its efficiency in game development.

- Physics engine: Built-in support for both 2D and 3D physics, enabling realistic game interactions.

- **Best Use Cases**:
  - Ideal for both **2D and 3D games** of all types (mobile, desktop, VR).
  - Best for **cross-platform games**, especially for games targeting both **mobile and console** markets.

- **Example**: Simple Unity 2D Game (C#):

```csharp
using UnityEngine;

public class PlayerController : MonoBehaviour
{
    public float speed = 5f;

    void Update()
    {
        float horizontal = Input.GetAxis("Horizontal");
        float vertical = Input.GetAxis("Vertical");
```

```
Vector3     movement    =     new
Vector3(horizontal, 0f, vertical) * speed
* Time.deltaTime;
        transform.Translate(movement);
   }
}
```

This code enables basic movement for a 2D player in Unity using the **Input system** and **C# scripting**.

2. Pygame (Python)

Pygame is a set of **Python modules** designed for **game development**. It's particularly useful for small-scale games and prototyping, and while it's not as feature-rich as Unity for complex 3D games, it's perfect for building **2D games** quickly and easily.

- **Key Features**:
    - **Simplicity**: Pygame's API is simple and easy to understand, making it a good choice for beginners.
    - **2D game development**: Pygame excels at creating **2D games**, with a focus on pixel-based graphics, sprite animations, and sound.

- o **Python integration**: Pygame integrates seamlessly with Python, a language known for its ease of use and vast ecosystem.
- o **No built-in physics engine**: Unlike Unity, Pygame doesn't come with a built-in physics engine, which means you will need to write your own logic or use external libraries for physics simulations.

- **Best Use Cases**:
  - o Ideal for **2D games** and quick prototypes.
  - o Best for learning game development or creating simple games that don't require advanced 3D features.

- **Example**: Simple Pygame 2D Game (Python):

```python
import pygame

pygame.init()
screen = pygame.display.set_mode((800, 600))
clock = pygame.time.Clock()

player = pygame.Rect(400, 300, 50, 50)
speed = 5
```

191

```python
while True:
    for event in pygame.event.get():
        if event.type == pygame.QUIT:
            pygame.quit()
            exit()

    keys = pygame.key.get_pressed()
    if keys[pygame.K_LEFT]:
        player.x -= speed
    if keys[pygame.K_RIGHT]:
        player.x += speed
    if keys[pygame.K_UP]:
        player.y -= speed
    if keys[pygame.K_DOWN]:
        player.y += speed

    screen.fill((0, 0, 0))
    pygame.draw.rect(screen, (255, 0, 0),
player)
    pygame.display.flip()
    clock.tick(60)
```

This basic **Pygame** example demonstrates how to move a **rectangle** (player character) around the screen using arrow keys.

14.2 Building Cross-Platform 2D and 3D Games

Let's now explore how to create **cross-platform 2D and 3D games** using **Unity (C#)** and **Pygame (Python)**.

1. 2D Game Development with Unity (C#)

Unity's built-in support for **2D game development** includes tools for **sprite management**, **2D physics**, and **tilemaps**. Here's how you would approach building a basic 2D game in Unity:

- **Create a new 2D project** in Unity.
- **Add 2D sprites** for characters, obstacles, and backgrounds.
- Use **Unity's physics engine** for character movement, collision detection, and interactions.
- Add **UI elements** for score, health, and other information.
- **Export to multiple platforms** (iOS, Android, PC, etc.).

2. 2D Game Development with Pygame

Pygame is well-suited for creating **2D games**, and it gives you direct control over the rendering process. Here's how to create a simple 2D game with **Pygame**:

- **Load 2D sprites** for characters and obstacles.
- Use **Pygame's event loop** to handle user input (keyboard, mouse).
- Implement **collision detection** manually or with external libraries.
- **Handle game states** (e.g., start, game over, restart).

3. 3D Game Development with Unity (C#)

Unity's 3D game development tools are robust and powerful. Here's an overview of creating a **3D game**:

- **Create a new 3D project** in Unity.
- **Design 3D models** using Unity's built-in **ProBuilder** tool or import assets from other tools (e.g., **Blender**).
- Use Unity's **Physics engine** for realistic movements, gravity, and collision detection.
- Set up a **camera system** for player perspective and control.
- Export to **3D platforms** like **PC**, **Consoles**, and **Mobile**.

4. 3D Game Development with Pygame

Pygame is **not inherently suited for 3D game development**, but you can achieve simple 3D graphics using libraries like **PyOpenGL**. If you want a more advanced 3D game engine, consider using **Godot** (which supports Python scripting) or Unity with **C#**.

14.3 Real-World Example: Creating a Multiplayer Game Prototype

Let's create a **multiplayer game prototype** using Unity (C#) and Photon, a popular multiplayer framework for Unity. This prototype will allow two players to join the same game and interact with each other.

1. Setting Up Unity for Multiplayer

- **Install Photon**: First, install the **Photon Unity Networking (PUN)** package from the Unity Asset Store.
- **Create a New Unity Project**: Start with a **2D or 3D game** template and import the Photon package.
- **Set Up Photon**:

195

o   Create a **Photon Cloud** account.

o   Add your **App ID** to the Photon settings in Unity.

2. Writing the Multiplayer Code

Here's an example of a simple multiplayer game setup in Unity using **Photon**:

- **Connect to Photon**:

csharp

```
using Photon.Pun;

public class GameManager :
MonoBehaviourPunCallbacks
{
    void Start()
    {

PhotonNetwork.ConnectUsingSettings();
    }

    public override void
OnConnectedToMaster()
    {
        PhotonNetwork.JoinLobby();
    }
```

```csharp
public override void OnJoinedLobby()
{
    PhotonNetwork.JoinRandomRoom();
}

public override void
OnJoinRandomFailed(short returnCode,
string message)
{
    PhotonNetwork.CreateRoom(null, new
Photon.Realtime.RoomOptions());
}
}
```

- **Player Script**:

```csharp
csharp

using Photon.Pun;
using UnityEngine;

public class PlayerController :
MonoBehaviourPun
{
    void Update()
    {
        if (photonView.IsMine)
        {
            float horizontal =
Input.GetAxis("Horizontal");
```

197

```
        float        vertical        =
Input.GetAxis("Vertical");

            Vector3   movement   =   new
Vector3(horizontal,    0,    vertical)    *
Time.deltaTime;

transform.Translate(movement);
        }
    }
}
```

- **Synchronizing Player Movement**: The `photonView.IsMine` check ensures that only the local player can control their own character. Photon handles synchronizing the movement of other players.

3. Testing the Multiplayer Game

1. **Build the game** for both iOS and Android (or desktop platforms).
2. **Test the game** by running two instances of the game on different devices or windows.
3. **Join the game** and interact with the other player in real time.

Conclusion

In this chapter, we explored **game development** with **Python** and **C#**, comparing **Unity** and **Pygame** for creating **2D and 3D games**. We walked through a **hands-on project** to build a **multiplayer game prototype** and discussed key aspects of **cross-platform development**, including how to deploy games for multiple platforms and implement multiplayer functionality using tools like **Photon**.

In the next chapter, we will dive deeper into **game performance optimization** and **real-time networking** strategies for creating smooth and responsive multiplayer experiences.

Let's continue building! 🚀

Chapter 15

Secure Coding Practices for Python and C#

Security is a critical aspect of application development, and it's essential for developers to follow **secure coding practices** to safeguard applications from various vulnerabilities. In this chapter, we will explore how to avoid common security flaws, such as **SQL Injection**, **XSS**, and **CSRF** in both **Python** and **C#**. We will also discuss secure authentication methods, focusing on **OAuth 2.0** and **JWT**. Lastly, we will walk through a **case study** of **building a secure login system**.

15.1 Avoiding Common Security Flaws

Understanding and preventing common security flaws is essential for building secure applications. Below are some of

200

the most common vulnerabilities and how to mitigate them in **Python** and **C#**.

SQL injection occurs when an attacker can manipulate an SQL query to execute arbitrary SQL code in the backend database, leading to data theft, loss, or corruption. It usually happens when **user inputs** are directly included in SQL queries without proper sanitization.

- **Prevention in Python (with SQLAlchemy)**: Always use **parameterized queries** to prevent SQL injection.

  Example using **SQLAlchemy**:

  ```python
  from sqlalchemy.orm import sessionmaker
  from sqlalchemy import create_engine

  engine =
  create_engine('sqlite:///example.db')
  Session = sessionmaker(bind=engine)
  session = Session()

  # Safe query with parameters
  ```

```
user_id = '123'
result = session.execute("SELECT * FROM
users WHERE id = :id", {'id': user_id})
```

- **Prevention in C# (with Entity Framework)**: Use **LINQ** or **parameterized queries** in **Entity Framework** to safely handle user input.

  Example:

  ```csharp
  using (var context = new MyDbContext())
  {
      string userId = "123";
      var user = context.Users.Where(u =>
  u.Id == userId).FirstOrDefault();
  }
  ```

2. Cross-Site Scripting (XSS)

XSS attacks allow an attacker to inject malicious scripts into web pages that other users view. These scripts can steal cookies, hijack sessions, or perform actions on behalf of the user.

- **Prevention in Python (Flask/Django)**: Always **escape output** that comes from untrusted sources, and never insert raw user input directly into HTML.

In **Flask**, use **Jinja2** templating, which automatically escapes content:

```html
html
```

```html
<p>{{ user_input }}</p> <!-- Safe from XSS
-->
```

- **Prevention in C# (ASP.NET Core)**: In **ASP.NET Core**, the **Razor view engine** automatically escapes data in views by default.

  Example:

  ```csharp
  csharp
  ```

  ```csharp
  <p>@userInput</p> <!-- Safe from XSS -->
  ```

  Always use **HTML sanitization** libraries like **HtmlSanitizer** in .NET when needed.

3. Cross-Site Request Forgery (CSRF)

CSRF allows attackers to perform actions on behalf of an authenticated user without their consent, usually by tricking the user into clicking a malicious link.

- **Prevention in Python (Flask/Django)**: Use CSRF tokens in forms to prevent unauthorized requests. Both **Flask** and **Django** offer built-in protections.

  o **Django**: Django has CSRF protection enabled by default. Ensure the `{% csrf_token %}` template tag is included in every form:

  html

  ```
  <form method="POST">
      {% csrf_token %}
      <!-- form fields -->
  </form>
  ```

  o **Flask**: Use the **Flask-WTF** extension for handling CSRF protection:

  python

  ```
  from flask_wtf import FlaskForm
  class MyForm(FlaskForm):
      # form fields here
  ```

- **Prevention in C# (ASP.NET Core)**: **ASP.NET Core** also provides **built-in CSRF protection**.

Ensure   that   forms   use   the
`@Html.AntiForgeryToken()` helper.

Example:

```
csharp
```

```
<form method="post">
    @Html.AntiForgeryToken()
    <!-- form fields -->
</form>
```

15.2 Secure Authentication: OAuth 2.0 and JWT

Secure authentication is critical to ensuring that only authorized users can access sensitive resources. **OAuth 2.0** and **JWT (JSON Web Tokens)** are widely used methods for secure, stateless authentication.

1. OAuth 2.0

OAuth 2.0 is an authorization framework that allows third-party applications to access a user's resources without exposing credentials. It is often used for **social logins** (e.g., signing in with Google or Facebook).

- **Flow of OAuth 2.0**:
  1. The user is redirected to the **authorization server** to authenticate.
  2. After successful authentication, the **authorization server** issues an **authorization code**.
  3. The client exchanges the code for an **access token**.
  4. The **access token** is used to access the user's resources.
- **Example in Python (using Authlib)**:

python

```
from      authlib.integrations.flask_client
import OAuth
app = Flask(__name__)
oauth = OAuth(app)

google = oauth.register(
    name='google',
    client_id='YOUR_GOOGLE_CLIENT_ID',
```

```
client_secret='YOUR_GOOGLE_CLIENT_SECRET'
,

authorize_url='https://accounts.google.co
m/o/oauth2/auth',
    authorize_params=None,

access_token_url='https://accounts.google
.com/o/oauth2/token',
    refresh_token_url=None,
    client_kwargs={'scope':        'openid
profile email'}
)
```

- **Example in C# (using OAuth2.0 with ASP.NET Core)**: In **ASP.NET Core**, you can configure OAuth with external providers like Google or Facebook by adding the necessary services:

csharp

```csharp
public                              void
ConfigureServices(IServiceCollection
services)
{
    services.AddAuthentication(options =>
    {
```

```
        options.DefaultScheme           =
CookieAuthenticationDefaults.Authenticati
onScheme;
        options.DefaultChallengeScheme   =
GoogleDefaults.AuthenticationScheme;
    })
    .AddGoogle(options =>
    {
        options.ClientId                 =
"YOUR_GOOGLE_CLIENT_ID";
        options.ClientSecret             =
"YOUR_GOOGLE_CLIENT_SECRET";
    });
}
```

2. JWT (JSON Web Tokens)

JWT is a compact, URL-safe token used for securely transmitting information between parties as a JSON object. JWTs are typically used for **stateless authentication** and authorization.

- **How JWT Works**:
    1. The client sends a request to the authentication server with credentials.
    2. The server authenticates the user and issues a **JWT**.

3. The client stores the **JWT** (usually in localStorage) and includes it in the **Authorization header** of future requests.

- **Example in Python (using PyJWT)**:

```python
python

import jwt
from datetime import datetime, timedelta

secret_key = 'your_secret_key'

def create_token(user_id):
    expiration = datetime.utcnow() + timedelta(hours=1)
    payload = {'user_id': user_id, 'exp': expiration}
    return jwt.encode(payload, secret_key, algorithm='HS256')

def decode_token(token):
    return jwt.decode(token, secret_key, algorithms=['HS256'])
```

- **Example in C# (using JWT.Net)**:

```csharp
csharp

using System;
```

```
using JWT;
using JWT.Algorithms;
using JWT.Serializers;

public class JwtHelper
{
    public          static          string
GenerateToken(string userId)
    {
        var payload = new
        {
            user_id = userId,
            exp                          =
DateTime.UtcNow.AddHours(1)
        };

        IJwtAlgorithm   algorithm   =   new
HMACSHA256Algorithm();
        IJsonSerializer   serializer   =   new
JsonNetSerializer();
        IDateTimeProvider   provider   =   new
UtcDateTimeProvider();
        IJwtEncoder      encoder      =      new
JwtEncoder(algorithm,           serializer,
provider);

        return      encoder.Encode(payload,
"your_secret_key");
    }
```

```
public          static          void
ValidateToken(string token)
    {
        var decoder = new JwtDecoder();
        var      payload      =
decoder.DecodeToObject(token,
"your_secret_key", verify: true);
    }
}
```

15.3 Case Study: Building a Secure Login System

Let's put these concepts together in a **case study** where we build a **secure login system** using **OAuth 2.0** and **JWT**. This system will authenticate users and issue a **JWT** for authorization.

1. Python (Flask)

We will use **Flask** and **Authlib** for OAuth 2.0 authentication and **PyJWT** for generating the JWT.

- **Setup Flask**:

211

```bash
bash

pip install Flask Authlib PyJWT
```

- **Code for Flask Login System**:

```python
python

from flask import Flask, redirect, url_for,
session
from     authlib.integrations.flask_client
import OAuth
import jwt

app = Flask(__name__)
app.secret_key = 'your_secret_key'
oauth = OAuth(app)

google = oauth.register(
    name='google',
    client_id='YOUR_GOOGLE_CLIENT_ID',

client_secret='YOUR_GOOGLE_CLIENT_SECRET'
,

authorize_url='https://accounts.google.co
m/o/oauth2/auth',

access_token_url='https://accounts.google
.com/o/oauth2/token',
```

```python
    client_kwargs={'scope':          'openid
profile email'}
)


@app.route('/')
def home():
    return 'Home Page'


@app.route('/login')
def login():
    return
google.authorize_redirect(url_for('auth',
_external=True))


@app.route('/auth')
def auth():
    token                            =
google.authorize_access_token()
    user_info                        =
google.parse_id_token(token)
    session['user'] = user_info
    jwt_token   =   jwt.encode({'user_id':
user_info['sub']},        'your_secret_key',
algorithm='HS256')
    return f'JWT Token: {jwt_token}'


if __name__ == '__main__':
    app.run(debug=True)
```

2. C# (ASP.NET Core)

In **ASP.NET Core**, we can configure **OAuth 2.0** using the built-in authentication middleware and issue a **JWT** using the **System.IdentityModel.Tokens.Jwt** library.

- **Setup ASP.NET Core**:

bash

```
dotnet add package
Microsoft.AspNetCore.Authentication.JwtBe
arer
```

- **Code for Secure Login System**:

csharp

```
public void
ConfigureServices(IServiceCollection
services)
{
    services.AddAuthentication(options =>
    {
        options.DefaultScheme =
CookieAuthenticationDefaults.Authenticati
onScheme;
        options.DefaultChallengeScheme =
GoogleDefaults.AuthenticationScheme;
```

214

```
    })
    .AddGoogle(options =>
    {
        options.ClientId              =
"YOUR_GOOGLE_CLIENT_ID";
        options.ClientSecret          =
"YOUR_GOOGLE_CLIENT_SECRET";
    });

    services.AddAuthorization();
}

public IActionResult Login()
{
    var token = GenerateJwtToken(user);
    return Ok(new { token });
}

private string GenerateJwtToken(User user)
{
    var claims = new[]
    {
        new           Claim(ClaimTypes.Name,
user.Username),
        new
Claim(ClaimTypes.NameIdentifier,
user.Id.ToString())
    };
```

215

```
var        key        =        new
SymmetricSecurityKey(Encoding.UTF8.GetByt
es("your_secret_key"));
    var        creds      =        new
SigningCredentials(key,
SecurityAlgorithms.HmacSha256);

    var token = new JwtSecurityToken(
        issuer: "your_app",
        audience: "your_app",
        claims: claims,
        expires: DateTime.Now.AddHours(1),
        signingCredentials: creds
    );

    return                           new
JwtSecurityTokenHandler().WriteToken(toke
n);
    }
```

Conclusion

In this chapter, we explored **secure coding practices** to help
protect your applications from common vulnerabilities like
SQL Injection, **XSS**, and **CSRF**. We also learned how to
implement **OAuth 2.0** and **JWT** for secure authentication.
Finally, we built a **secure login system** in both **Python**

(Flask) and **C# (ASP.NET Core)**, showcasing how to implement these best practices in a real-world scenario.

In the next chapter, we will dive into **performance optimization** for both **Python** and **C#** applications to ensure your app runs efficiently under load.

Let's continue building! 🚀

Chapter 16

Performance Optimization in Python and C#

Performance optimization is crucial for ensuring that your applications run efficiently and can handle high traffic without degrading user experience. In this chapter, we will discuss **optimizing code execution for speed and efficiency** in **Python** and **C#**. We will explore how to implement **asynchronous programming** using **async/await** to handle I/O-bound tasks and scale applications effectively. Lastly, we will work through a **real-world example** of **optimizing an API for high traffic**.

16.1 Optimizing Code Execution for Speed and Efficiency

Optimizing your code for speed and efficiency typically involves reducing resource consumption (memory, CPU) and improving response time. Let's look at some key strategies for optimizing code in **Python** and **C#**.

1. Optimizing Code in Python

- **Profiling Code**: Start by profiling your code to identify performance bottlenecks. You can use **cProfile** and **timeit** to understand where the code is slow.

  Example using **cProfile**:

  ```python
  import cProfile

  def slow_function():
      total = 0
      for i in range(1, 1000000):
          total += i
      return total

  cProfile.run('slow_function()')
  ```

- **Use Built-in Functions**: Python's built-in functions (like `sum()`, `map()`, `filter()`) are written in **C** and are optimized for speed. Use them instead of writing custom loops.

- **Avoid Global Variables**: Accessing global variables is slower than accessing local variables. Minimize the use of global variables and pass variables explicitly to functions.

- **Efficient Data Structures**: Use appropriate data structures to optimize performance. For example, use **sets** for membership tests rather than **lists**, as set lookups are generally faster.

- **List Comprehensions**: List comprehensions are generally faster than using **for loops** in Python.

Example:

```python
numbers = [i for i in range(1000)]
```

2. Optimizing Code in C#

- **Profiling Code**: In C#, use **Visual Studio's Performance Profiler** or **BenchmarkDotNet** to identify performance bottlenecks.

Example with **BenchmarkDotNet**:

```csharp
using BenchmarkDotNet.Attributes;
```

```
using BenchmarkDotNet.Running;

public class MyBenchmark
{
    [Benchmark]
    public int SlowFunction()
    {
        int total = 0;
        for (int i = 0; i < 1000000; i++)
        {
            total += i;
        }
        return total;
    }
}

class Program
{
    static void Main()
    {
        var            summary           =
BenchmarkRunner.Run<MyBenchmark>();
    }
}
```

- **Use Value Types (Structs)**: Prefer **value types (structs)** over **reference types (classes)** for small data structures, as value types are allocated on the stack and are more efficient.

- **String Concatenation**: Avoid using + for string concatenation in loops. Use **StringBuilder** instead for better performance.

Example:

```csharp
csharp

StringBuilder sb = new StringBuilder();
for (int i = 0; i < 1000; i++)
{
    sb.Append(i);
}
string result = sb.ToString();
```

- **Avoid LINQ in Hot Paths**: While LINQ provides concise and readable code, it may incur performance overhead. If performance is critical in time-sensitive sections of the code, avoid LINQ and use traditional loops.

16.2 Asynchronous Programming with async/await

Asynchronous programming is crucial for improving the performance of **I/O-bound tasks** (e.g., reading from files, querying a database, making HTTP requests). By using **async/await**, you can write non-blocking code that can handle multiple tasks concurrently without waiting for each one to finish.

1. Asynchronous Programming in Python (asyncio)

Python provides **asyncio** as a built-in library for handling asynchronous programming. Use **async/await** syntax to define asynchronous functions and manage concurrency.

- **Basic AsyncIO Example**:

```python
python

import asyncio

async def fetch_data(url):
    print(f"Fetching data from {url}")
    await asyncio.sleep(2)  # Simulate I/O-
bound task
    print(f"Data fetched from {url}")
    return f"Data from {url}"

async def main():
    tasks = [
```

```
fetch_data('https://example1.com'),

fetch_data('https://example2.com'),

fetch_data('https://example3.com')
    ]
    results = await asyncio.gather(*tasks)
    print(results)

asyncio.run(main())
```

- **Key Points**:
  - o **async def** defines an asynchronous function.
  - o **await** is used to pause the function's execution while waiting for an asynchronous task to complete.
  - o **asyncio.gather** is used to run multiple asynchronous tasks concurrently.

2. Asynchronous Programming in C# (async/await)

In C#, the **async/await** pattern is part of the language and is supported by .NET libraries, making it easy to write non-blocking code.

- **Basic Async/Await Example**:

```
csharp

using System;
using System.Threading.Tasks;

class Program
{
    static       async       Task<string>
FetchDataAsync(string url)
    {
        Console.WriteLine($"Fetching  data
from {url}");
        await   Task.Delay(2000);      //
Simulate I/O-bound task
        Console.WriteLine($"Data    fetched
from {url}");
        return $"Data from {url}";
    }

    static async Task Main(string[] args)
    {
        Task<string>        task1      =
FetchDataAsync("https://example1.com");
        Task<string>        task2      =
FetchDataAsync("https://example2.com");
        Task<string>        task3      =
FetchDataAsync("https://example3.com");
```

225

```
        string[]   results   =   await
Task.WhenAll(task1, task2, task3);
        foreach (var result in results)
        {
            Console.WriteLine(result);
        }
    }
}
```

- **Key Points**:
    - ○ **async Task** defines an asynchronous method that returns a **Task** (or **Task<T>**).
    - ○ **await** is used to wait for an asynchronous task to complete, allowing other tasks to run concurrently.
    - ○ **Task.WhenAll** is used to run multiple asynchronous tasks concurrently and wait for all to complete.

16.3 Real-World Example: Optimizing an API for High Traffic

Now, let's walk through optimizing an **API** to handle **high traffic** using **asynchronous programming**. In this case, we'll look at a simple API that fetches data from a database and then sends the data to the client. The goal is to improve performance to handle a large number of concurrent requests without blocking threads.

1. Optimizing in Python with FastAPI (async/await)

FastAPI is a modern, fast web framework for building APIs in Python, and it supports asynchronous programming out of the box.

- **FastAPI Example (Optimized)**:

```python
from fastapi import FastAPI
import asyncio

app = FastAPI()

async def fetch_data_from_db(query):
    await asyncio.sleep(1)    # Simulate
database call
    return f"Results for query: {query}"

@app.get("/data/{query}")
async def get_data(query: str):
    data = await fetch_data_from_db(query)
```

```
return {"data": data}
```

- **Explanation**:
  - **asyncio.sleep** is used to simulate an asynchronous database call.
  - The **FastAPI** route handler is asynchronous, allowing the server to handle other requests while waiting for the data.

2. Optimizing in C# with ASP.NET Core (async/await)

In **ASP.NET Core**, we can optimize the API by using **async/await** for database calls and I/O-bound operations.

- **ASP.NET Core Example (Optimized)**:

```csharp
using Microsoft.AspNetCore.Mvc;
using System.Threading.Tasks;

[ApiController]
[Route("api/[controller]")]
public class DataController :
ControllerBase
{
    private readonly IDataService
_dataService;
```

```csharp
    public      DataController(IDataService
dataService)
    {
        _dataService = dataService;
    }

    [HttpGet("{query}")]
    public   async    Task<IActionResult>
GetData(string query)
    {
        var      data      =      await
_dataService.FetchDataFromDbAsync(query);
        return Ok(new { data });
    }
}

public interface IDataService
{
    Task<string>
FetchDataFromDbAsync(string query);
}

public class DataService : IDataService
{
    public      async      Task<string>
FetchDataFromDbAsync(string query)
    {
```

```
        await      Task.Delay(1000);      //
Simulate database call
        return    $"Results    for    query:
{query}";
    }
}
```

- **Explanation**:
  - ○ **Task.Delay** simulates a database call that runs asynchronously.
  - ○ The controller's **GetData** method is asynchronous, allowing the server to handle other requests while fetching data from the database.

Conclusion

In this chapter, we learned about **performance optimization** in both **Python** and **C#**. We covered **optimizing code execution** for speed and efficiency, including using **profiling tools** and **efficient data structures**. We also explored **asynchronous programming** with **async/await** to handle **I/O-bound tasks** more efficiently. Finally, we walked through a **real-world example** of optimizing an API for high traffic, making it scalable and responsive under load.

In the next chapter, we will delve into **scalable architectures** and how to design systems that can handle increasing loads while maintaining performance.

Let's continue building! 🚀

Chapter 17

DevOps and CI/CD Pipelines

In modern software development, **DevOps** practices have become crucial for automating workflows, improving collaboration between development and operations teams, and ensuring **continuous integration (CI)** and **continuous delivery (CD)**. In this chapter, we will explore how to **automate deployments** using popular tools like **GitHub Actions, Azure DevOps**, and **Jenkins**. We will also walk through a **hands-on example** of setting up **CI/CD for a cloud-based web app** and discuss how to monitor applications with **Prometheus, ELK Stack**, and **Azure Monitor**.

17.1 Automating Deployments with GitHub Actions, Azure DevOps, Jenkins

The goal of DevOps is to ensure that software is delivered quickly and reliably, and CI/CD pipelines are central to this process. Let's take a closer look at three major CI/CD tools: **GitHub Actions**, **Azure DevOps**, and **Jenkins**.

1. GitHub Actions

GitHub Actions is a powerful automation tool integrated into **GitHub** repositories. It allows you to automate the build, test, and deployment process directly within your **GitHub repository**.

- **Key Features**:
    o Native **integration with GitHub repositories**.
    o Supports **YAML-based configuration** for defining workflows.
    o Easily integrates with third-party services and APIs.
- **Example: CI/CD with GitHub Actions**: Below is a simple **GitHub Actions** workflow configuration (`.github/workflows/ci-cd.yml`) for a **Node.js** application:

```yaml
yaml

name: CI/CD Pipeline
```

```
on:
  push:
    branches:
      - main

jobs:
  build:
    runs-on: ubuntu-latest

    steps:
      - name: Checkout code
        uses: actions/checkout@v2

      - name: Set up Node.js
        uses: actions/setup-node@v2
        with:
          node-version: '14'

      - name: Install dependencies
        run: npm install

      - name: Run tests
        run: npm test

      - name: Deploy to AWS
        run: |
```

```
        aws         configure        set
aws_access_key_id                    ${{
secrets.AWS_ACCESS_KEY_ID }}
        aws         configure        set
aws_secret_access_key                ${{
secrets.AWS_SECRET_ACCESS_KEY }}
        aws  s3  sync  ./dist  s3://my-
bucket-name
        env:
        AWS_ACCESS_KEY_ID:           ${{
secrets.AWS_ACCESS_KEY_ID }}
        AWS_SECRET_ACCESS_KEY:       ${{
secrets.AWS_SECRET_ACCESS_KEY }}
```

- **Explanation**:

  o **Checkout code**: Fetches the code from the GitHub repository.

  o **Set up Node.js**: Specifies the Node.js version for the build.

  o **Install dependencies**: Installs the app dependencies.

  o **Run tests**: Runs the tests to ensure code quality.

  o **Deploy to AWS**: Deploys the application to **AWS S3** using AWS CLI commands.

2. Azure DevOps

Azure DevOps is a comprehensive set of tools for managing the software lifecycle, providing CI/CD pipelines, version control, and project management. It integrates well with **Azure** services and can deploy applications to various environments.

- **Key Features**:
    - ○ **Integrated** with Azure services like **App Services, Kubernetes**, and **Azure Functions**.
    - ○ Supports **YAML-based pipeline definitions** and **visual editors** for pipeline creation.
    - ○ Handles **CI/CD, build automation, release management**, and more.
- **Example: CI/CD Pipeline in Azure DevOps**: A simple Azure DevOps YAML pipeline for a **.NET Core** application:

```yaml
trigger:
  branches:
    include:
      - main

pool:
```

```
    vmImage: 'windows-latest'

steps:
  - task: UseDotNet@2
    inputs:
      packageType: 'sdk'
      version: '5.x'
      installationPath:
$(Agent.ToolsDirectory)/dotnet

  - task: DotNetCoreCLI@2
    inputs:
      command: restore
      projects: '**/*.csproj'

  - task: DotNetCoreCLI@2
    inputs:
      command: build
      projects: '**/*.csproj'

  - task: DotNetCoreCLI@2
    inputs:
      command: publish
      publishWebProjects: true
      arguments: '--configuration Release
--output
$(Build.ArtifactStagingDirectory)/publish
'
```

```
- task: AzureWebApp@1
  inputs:
    appName: 'my-app-service'
    package:
'$(Build.ArtifactStagingDirectory)/publis
h'
```

- **Explanation**:
  - o The pipeline restores dependencies, builds the app, publishes the output, and deploys it to **Azure Web App**.
  - o You can modify this pipeline to deploy to other Azure services like **App Service** or **Kubernetes**.

3. Jenkins

Jenkins is one of the most widely used open-source tools for continuous integration and delivery. It allows you to automate various stages of the software development lifecycle, such as building, testing, and deploying applications.

- **Key Features**:
  - o Extensible with a wide variety of **plugins**.
  - o **Supports complex pipeline configurations** with **Jenkinsfile**.

238

- o Can be used with any version control system, not just GitHub.

- **Example: CI/CD Pipeline in Jenkins**: A basic **Jenkinsfile** to automate the CI/CD process for a **Java** application:

```groovy
pipeline {
    agent any

    environment {
        DEPLOYMENT_DIR                    =
'/home/jenkins/deploy'
    }

    stages {
        stage('Build') {
            steps {
                script {
                    echo    'Building    the
application...'
                    sh    './mvnw    clean
package'
                }
            }
        }

        stage('Test') {
```

239

```
            steps {
                script {
                    echo            'Running
tests...'
                    sh './mvnw test'
                }
            }
        }

        stage('Deploy') {
            steps {
                script {
                    echo  'Deploying  the
application...'
                    sh              'scp
target/myapp.jar
user@server:/path/to/deploy'
                }
            }
        }
    }

    post {
        always {
            echo 'Cleaning up...'
        }
    }
}
```

• **Explanation**:

- o **Build**: This stage builds the application using **Maven**.
- o **Test**: This stage runs the tests using **Maven**.
- o **Deploy**: This stage deploys the application to a remote server using **SCP**.

17.2 Hands-On Example: Setting Up CI/CD for a Cloud-Based Web App

In this section, we will walk through setting up a **CI/CD pipeline** for a cloud-based web app, using **GitHub Actions** for continuous integration and **Azure DevOps** for deployment.

1. Setting Up CI with GitHub Actions

We already explored a **GitHub Actions** workflow above. To create a CI pipeline:

1. **Create a repository** for your web app on **GitHub**.
2. **Add a** `.github/workflows/ci.yml` **file** to the root of the repository, with the workflow definition as discussed earlier.

3. **Push code changes** to the **main branch**, and GitHub Actions will automatically trigger the pipeline.

2. Setting Up CD with Azure DevOps

For deployment:

1. **Create an Azure DevOps organization** and a new **project**.
2. **Link your GitHub repository** to Azure DevOps and set up a **YAML pipeline** similar to the one above.
3. **Configure the pipeline** to deploy to Azure App Service or another cloud platform as needed.

17.3 Monitoring with Prometheus, ELK Stack, Azure Monitor

Once your application is deployed, it's important to monitor its performance, logs, and health. Let's explore some popular monitoring tools.

1. Prometheus

Prometheus is an open-source monitoring tool used for collecting time-series data. It can scrape metrics from applications and services.

- **Set up Prometheus** to monitor your app:
    - **Install Prometheus** and **Grafana**.
    - Configure Prometheus to scrape metrics from your app endpoints.
    - Set up alerts and dashboards in **Grafana** for real-time monitoring.

Example of exposing metrics in a Python app using **Prometheus client**:

python

```python
from prometheus_client import start_http_server,
Summary

REQUESTS = Summary('requests_total', 'Total
number of requests')

@app.route('/metrics')
@REQUESTS.count_exceptions()
def metrics():
    return generate_latest()
```

243

2. ELK Stack

The **ELK Stack** (Elasticsearch, Logstash, and Kibana) is used for logging and visualizing logs. It helps you collect, analyze, and visualize logs from your applications.

- **Logstash** collects and processes logs from different sources.
- **Elasticsearch** stores and indexes log data.
- **Kibana** visualizes the data and allows for interactive querying.

3. Azure Monitor

Azure Monitor is a comprehensive solution for collecting, analyzing, and acting on telemetry data from your Azure applications and services.

- **Set up Azure Monitor** to track metrics, logs, and application health.
- **Configure Application Insights** to collect telemetry data from your app, including performance metrics, failures, and usage.

Conclusion

In this chapter, we explored how to automate deployments with **GitHub Actions**, **Azure DevOps**, and **Jenkins**. We walked through a hands-on example of setting up **CI/CD for a cloud-based web app** and discussed how to monitor applications using **Prometheus**, **ELK Stack**, and **Azure Monitor**. These tools help ensure that your applications are continuously integrated, delivered, and monitored effectively, enabling you to catch issues early and deliver better software.

In the next chapter, we will explore **scalable architectures** and design patterns that can handle high loads and ensure long-term stability and performance.

Let's continue building! 🚀

Part 7

Emerging Technologies and the Future of Programming

Chapter 18

The Future of AI and Automation in Programming

The landscape of **software development** is evolving rapidly, with **AI** and **automation** playing an increasingly pivotal role in how developers write code, optimize processes, and enhance productivity. In this chapter, we will explore how **AI** is shaping the future of programming, focusing on **AI-assisted coding tools** like **GitHub Copilot**, **ChatGPT**, and **OpenAI Codex**. We will also work through a **real-world case study** to demonstrate how AI can assist developers in writing and optimizing code.

18.1 How AI is Shaping the Future of Software Development

AI is transforming nearly every field, and software development is no exception. AI technologies can automate repetitive tasks, assist with complex problem-solving, and even enhance creativity in the coding process. Some of the key ways in which AI is shaping the future of programming include:

1. Code Generation and Assistance

AI-driven tools are capable of **automating the generation of code** based on natural language instructions, saving developers time by providing intelligent code suggestions and completions. This helps programmers focus on **higher-level tasks**, such as designing features and solving business problems.

- **AI in IDEs**: Integrated Development Environments (IDEs) powered by AI can provide **contextual code suggestions**, refactor code, and highlight potential bugs in real-time, allowing developers to write more reliable and efficient code.

2. Automated Bug Detection and Code Optimization

AI can assist in detecting **bugs** and **optimizing code** by learning from vast amounts of codebases and identifying patterns that lead to issues or inefficiencies. AI models can suggest ways to improve code performance or point out common mistakes that would typically require manual code review.

- **Code analysis tools** can automatically identify areas of code that could benefit from **refactoring** or optimization, such as **reducing complexity, improving readability,** or **optimizing resource usage**.

3. Natural Language Processing (NLP) for Code Understanding

With **Natural Language Processing (NLP),** AI tools can interpret **plain English** (or other languages) to automatically generate code or understand code requirements. This enables developers to interact with their codebase using natural language, making the development process more intuitive and accessible.

4. AI-Driven Testing and Continuous Integration (CI)

AI can enhance the testing phase of software development by predicting which tests are likely to catch bugs, **automating test generation**, and analyzing test results more efficiently. With AI-assisted **Continuous Integration (CI),** testing cycles can be shortened, and code deployments can be automated with greater confidence in their stability.

18.2 The Rise of AI-Assisted Coding Tools

Several AI-assisted coding tools have emerged in recent years, revolutionizing how developers approach writing, testing, and optimizing code. Let's explore some of the most notable tools:

1. GitHub Copilot

GitHub Copilot is an AI-powered coding assistant developed by **GitHub** and **OpenAI**. It uses **OpenAI Codex**, an AI model trained on a vast corpus of programming languages, to provide **contextual code suggestions**.

- **Key Features**:
  - Autocompletes code based on comments and previous lines.
  - Provides full-function suggestions based on a brief description.
  - Can generate entire blocks of code, including libraries, algorithms, and data structures.

250

o Supports multiple languages, including **Python**, **JavaScript**, **Ruby**, **Go**, and more.

- **Example of GitHub Copilot in Action**: If a developer types a comment like:

```python

# Function to calculate the factorial of a number
```

GitHub Copilot might automatically generate the function:

```python

def factorial(n):
    if n == 0:
        return 1
    else:
        return n * factorial(n - 1)
```

2. ChatGPT

ChatGPT (created by OpenAI) is a **large language model** capable of understanding and generating human-like text based on the input it receives. ChatGPT can assist in programming by providing solutions, explaining code, or generating code snippets.

- **Key Features**:
  - o Offers **code suggestions** based on natural language queries.
  - o Can **explain code** to developers, making it easier to understand complex algorithms.
  - o Provides **debugging help** by suggesting ways to fix errors in code.
- **Example of ChatGPT**: You can ask ChatGPT:

```css
```

```
How do I implement a binary search
algorithm in Python?
```

ChatGPT will respond with a code snippet like:

```python
```

```python
def binary_search(arr, target):
    low, high = 0, len(arr) - 1
    while low <= high:
        mid = (low + high) // 2
        if arr[mid] == target:
            return mid
        elif arr[mid] < target:
            low = mid + 1
        else:
            high = mid - 1
```

```
return -1
```

3. OpenAI Codex

OpenAI Codex is the underlying AI model used in **GitHub Copilot**. Codex is trained on **billions of lines of code** and is capable of generating code in a variety of languages. It can assist in **writing functions**, **debugging code**, and even **translating code** from one language to another.

- **Key Features**:
    - Can generate code based on **natural language input**.
    - Understands a wide variety of **programming languages** and frameworks.
    - Can be used for complex programming tasks like **API integration** or **algorithm optimization**.

4. Tabnine

Tabnine is another AI-powered code completion tool that uses **machine learning** to provide intelligent code suggestions. Unlike Copilot, Tabnine is more focused on integrating with different IDEs and customizing itself to fit the unique workflows of teams and developers.

- **Key Features**:

- Uses AI to provide **real-time code completions**.
- Learns from a developer's past code and adapts to their style.
- Works with **IDE integrations** like **VS Code**, **JetBrains**, **Sublime Text**, and more.

18.3 Case Study: How AI Can Help Write and Optimize Code

Let's walk through a **real-world case study** where we use AI to write and optimize code for an application. Suppose we are building a **task management web app** with the following features:

- Add tasks.
- Mark tasks as complete.
- Delete tasks.
- View a list of all tasks.

We will use **AI-assisted coding tools** to help with the design of these features, improve code quality, and optimize performance.

1. Writing Code with GitHub Copilot

Using **GitHub Copilot**, we can quickly generate the necessary code for the **task management app**. For example, by typing the comment:

python

```
# Function to add a task to the database
```

GitHub Copilot might generate:

python

```
def add_task(task_name, db):
    task = Task(name=task_name, completed=False)
    db.session.add(task)
    db.session.commit()
    return task
```

2. Code Optimization with OpenAI Codex

After writing the initial code, we use **OpenAI Codex** to suggest optimizations. For instance, Codex could recommend improvements like reducing redundant database queries, improving error handling, or optimizing the user authentication process.

Before:

255

python

```python
def fetch_tasks(db):
    tasks                                    =
db.session.query(Task).filter_by(completed=Fals
e).all()
    return tasks
```

After Optimization:

python

```python
def fetch_tasks(db):
    # Using    indexed    queries    for    better
performance on large data sets
    tasks                                    =
db.session.query(Task).filter_by(completed=Fals
e).order_by(Task.created_at.desc()).limit(100).
all()
    return tasks
```

Here, Codex suggested ordering the tasks by creation date and limiting the result to the most recent 100 tasks, which improves both **performance** and **user experience**.

3. Debugging with ChatGPT

After implementing the features, we might run into an issue, such as a **bug** where tasks are not being marked as completed correctly. Instead of spending time trying to figure it out manually, we ask **ChatGPT** for help.

Question:

```
csharp
```

```
Why is my code not marking tasks as completed
when I click the "Mark as Completed" button?
```

ChatGPT provides a potential fix:

```
pgsql
```

```
The issue might be with how you're updating the
task status. Make sure that the changes are being
committed to the database after the update. You
should also check if there's an issue with your
form submission or the button event handler.
```

After applying the suggested fix, the issue is resolved, and tasks are correctly marked as complete.

Conclusion

In this chapter, we explored how **AI** is revolutionizing **software development** by assisting developers in writing, debugging, and optimizing code. We discussed how tools like **GitHub Copilot**, **ChatGPT**, and **OpenAI Codex** can significantly speed up the development process, enhance productivity, and improve code quality. Through a real-world case study, we saw how these tools can assist in building and optimizing an app, from generating code to solving bugs and optimizing performance.

As AI continues to advance, it will play an increasingly vital role in the **future of programming**, enabling developers to be more efficient and focus on solving higher-level problems rather than routine coding tasks.

In the next chapter, we will explore **emerging trends in quantum computing**, **blockchain**, and other futuristic technologies that will further shape the future of programming.

Let's continue building! 🚀

Chapter 19

Blockchain and Cloud Computing

Blockchain technology has revolutionized the way we think about data management, security, and trust. By enabling **decentralized applications** (dApps) and **smart contracts**, blockchain opens up new possibilities for businesses and developers. In this chapter, we will explore how to leverage **blockchain** for decentralized applications, delve into **smart contract development** using **Solidity** and **C#**, and provide a **case study** on integrating blockchain with **cloud storage** for enhanced security and reliability.

19.1 Using Blockchain for Decentralized Applications

Blockchain is a decentralized, distributed ledger technology that allows data to be stored across a network of computers, making it resistant to manipulation and fraud. Decentralized applications (dApps) are built on top of blockchain platforms and enable peer-to-peer interactions without relying on a central authority.

1. What is a Decentralized Application (dApp)?

A **dApp** is an application that runs on a blockchain or a decentralized network. Unlike traditional applications, which rely on central servers, dApps operate on peer-to-peer networks, providing transparency, security, and trustlessness.

- **Key Characteristics** of dApps:
  - **Decentralized**: The backend runs on a **blockchain** or decentralized network.
  - **Transparent**: Every action on the blockchain is public and verifiable.
  - **Autonomous**: They can run without human intervention through **smart contracts**.

2. Blockchain for Decentralized Applications

Blockchain is perfect for decentralized applications that require **trustless** interactions, such as **peer-to-peer transactions**, **financial services**, and **content sharing**. Some key platforms for building dApps include:

- **Ethereum**: A leading blockchain platform for building decentralized applications, primarily using **smart contracts**.
- **Binance Smart Chain (BSC)**: A fast and low-cost alternative to Ethereum for building decentralized applications.
- **Polkadot**: A multi-chain network that allows interoperability between different blockchains.
- **Solana**: Known for its high throughput and low-cost transactions.

By utilizing smart contracts, dApps can handle complex logic directly on the blockchain, enabling automation and security.

19.2 Building Smart Contracts with Solidity and C#

Smart contracts are self-executing contracts with the terms of the agreement directly written into code. They automatically enforce the execution of agreements when predefined conditions are met. Let's explore how to build and deploy **smart contracts** using **Solidity** (the primary language for Ethereum smart contracts) and **C#** (to interact with blockchain networks).

1. Smart Contracts with Solidity

Solidity is a programming language used to write smart contracts on the **Ethereum blockchain**. It is statically typed and similar to JavaScript, making it relatively easy to learn for developers familiar with web technologies.

- **Key Features of Solidity**:
  - **High-level language** designed for writing smart contracts.
  - Supports data structures such as **arrays**, **mappings**, and **structs**.
  - Allows interaction with other contracts and external data sources.
- **Simple Example: Smart Contract for a Token**

Here's a basic **Solidity** contract that implements an ERC-20 token (a standard for creating tokens on the Ethereum network):

```
solidity
```

```
// SPDX-License-Identifier: MIT
pragma solidity ^0.8.0;
```

```
contract SimpleToken {
    string public name = "Simple Token";
    string public symbol = "STK";
    uint8 public decimals = 18;
    uint256 public totalSupply;

    mapping(address    =>    uint256)    public
balanceOf;

    constructor(uint256 _initialSupply) {
        totalSupply    =    _initialSupply    *
10**uint256(decimals);
        balanceOf[msg.sender] = totalSupply;
    }

    function transfer(address recipient, uint256
amount) public returns (bool) {
        require(recipient    !=    address(0),
"Recipient address is invalid");
        require(balanceOf[msg.sender] >= amount,
"Insufficient balance");

        balanceOf[msg.sender] -= amount;
        balanceOf[recipient] += amount;
        return true;
    }
}
```

- **Explanation**:

263

- o This contract defines a **token** with a name, symbol, and initial supply.
- o It includes a `transfer` function to allow users to send tokens to other addresses.
- o The contract is deployed with an initial supply that is assigned to the creator of the contract.

2. Interacting with Blockchain Using C#

While Solidity is used to create smart contracts, **C#** is often used to interact with these contracts in decentralized applications. For C# developers, **Nethereum** is a .NET library that provides an easy way to interact with Ethereum and smart contracts.

- **Install Nethereum**:

```bash
Install-Package Nethereum.Web3
```

- **Example: Interacting with the Smart Contract in C#**:

Here's how to interact with the **SimpleToken** contract from a C# application:

```csharp
csharp

using Nethereum.Web3;
using Nethereum.Contracts;
using Nethereum.Hex.HexTypes;
using System;

class Program
{
    static async Task Main(string[] args)
    {
        string nodeUrl = "https://mainnet.infura.io/v3/YOUR_INFURA_PROJECT_ID";
        var web3 = new Web3(nodeUrl);

        string contractAddress = "0xYourContractAddress";
        string senderAddress = "0xYourAddress";

        // ABI of the SimpleToken contract
        string abi = "[{\"constant\":true,\"inputs\":[],\"name\":\"name\",\"outputs\":[{\"name\":\"\",\"type\":\"string\"}],\"payable\":false,\"stateMutability\":\"view\",\"type\":\"function\"}, ...]"; // truncated for brevity
```

```
      var          contract          =
web3.Eth.GetContract(abi,
contractAddress);
      var          nameFunction       =
contract.GetFunction("name");
      var     name      =      await
nameFunction.CallAsync<string>();

      Console.WriteLine($"Token    Name:
{name}");
    }
}
```

- **Explanation**:
  - o The **Nethereum.Web3** class is used to connect to the Ethereum network.
  - o We define the **ABI** (Application Binary Interface) for the contract and use it to interact with the **SimpleToken** contract.
  - o This C# application fetches the **token name** from the smart contract and displays it.

19.3 Case Study: Integrating Blockchain with Cloud Storage

Now, let's walk through a case study where we integrate **blockchain** with **cloud storage** to enhance **security** and **data redundancy**.

1. Scenario

Let's assume we are building a **document management system** that allows users to store documents securely in the cloud. We want to ensure that documents are tamper-proof and can be verified by anyone, even after being uploaded to the cloud. By using **blockchain** and **cloud storage**, we can achieve these goals.

2. Using Blockchain for Document Verification

- **Step 1: Document Upload**: When a user uploads a document, a **hash** of the document is created and stored on the blockchain.
- **Step 2: Cloud Storage**: The actual document is stored in a **cloud storage provider** like **Amazon S3** or **Azure Blob Storage**.
- **Step 3: Verification**: To verify a document's integrity, users can compare the hash stored on the blockchain with the hash of the document retrieved from the cloud.

- **Smart Contract for Document Storage**: The smart contract could store the **document hash** and the **timestamp** when the document was uploaded, providing a transparent and immutable record of when the document was stored.

Here's a simple **Solidity smart contract** to store the document hash:

```solidity

pragma solidity ^0.8.0;

contract DocumentStorage {
    struct Document {
        string documentHash;
        uint timestamp;
    }

    mapping(address => Document[]) public documents;

    function storeDocument(string memory documentHash) public {

documents[msg.sender].push(Document({
            documentHash: documentHash,
            timestamp: block.timestamp
```

```
        })));
    }

    function verifyDocument(address user,
string memory documentHash) public view
returns (bool) {
        for (uint i = 0; i <
documents[user].length; i++) {
            if
(keccak256(bytes(documents[user][i].docum
entHash))                        ==
keccak256(bytes(documentHash))) {
                return true;
            }
        }
        return false;
    }
}
```

- **Step 4: Interact with the Smart Contract from C#**: Using **Nethereum**, we can store and verify documents in the blockchain from a C# application, ensuring that any document uploaded to the cloud can be verified for integrity.

Conclusion

In this chapter, we explored how **blockchain** technology is transforming the development of **decentralized applications (dApps)** and enabling the creation of **smart contracts**. We learned how to write smart contracts using **Solidity** and interact with them using **C#** through the **Nethereum** library. Additionally, we demonstrated how to **integrate blockchain with cloud storage** to enhance **security** and **data integrity**.

Blockchain and cloud computing are converging to create more **secure**, **transparent**, and **trustworthy** systems for a variety of applications, from document management to financial services.

In the next chapter, we will explore **emerging trends in quantum computing** and how they may revolutionize computing in the future.

Let's continue building! 🚀

Chapter 20

Quantum Computing and Next-Generation Programming

Quantum computing is poised to revolutionize the world of computing by enabling solutions to problems that are currently beyond the capabilities of classical computers. As quantum hardware and algorithms continue to evolve, so does the need for developers to understand **quantum programming** and how it will impact existing software applications. In this chapter, we will explore **quantum programming with Q#**, discuss how quantum computing might affect **Python** and **C#** applications, and take a look at **future trends** in **hybrid cloud** and **quantum computing**.

20.1 Introduction to Quantum Programming with Q#

Quantum programming involves writing code for quantum computers, which operate based on the principles of quantum mechanics. **Q#** is a **quantum programming language** developed by **Microsoft** as part of the **Quantum Development Kit**. Q# is designed to run on quantum simulators or real quantum hardware, and it integrates with **.NET** frameworks, allowing developers familiar with **C#** to use quantum computing capabilities.

1. What is Q#?

Q# is a high-level language used to write **quantum algorithms**. It is used in conjunction with classical programming languages like **C#** or **Python**, which are responsible for classical computation. Q# provides a set of tools for **quantum operations, quantum measurements,** and **entanglement** — the key concepts of quantum mechanics that quantum computers exploit.

- **Key Features** of Q#:
    - ○ **Quantum operations**: Perform operations like **quantum gates** on quantum bits (qubits).
    - ○ **Classical-quantum integration**: Allows classical code (e.g., C#) to control quantum operations.
    - ○ **Simulation**: Run quantum algorithms on classical simulators to understand their behavior before deploying them to quantum hardware.

2. Quantum Concepts in Q#

- **Qubits**: Quantum bits that can exist in multiple states simultaneously due to **superposition**.
- **Entanglement**: A quantum phenomenon where two qubits become linked, such that the state of one qubit instantly affects the state of the other.
- **Quantum Gates**: Operators applied to qubits that alter their state. Examples include the **Hadamard gate** (creates superposition) and the **CNOT gate** (entangles two qubits).

3. Example of Quantum Programming with Q#

Here's a simple example of a **quantum program** written in Q# that creates a **superposition** of two qubits and then measures their state:

```qsharp
qsharp

namespace QuantumExample
{
    open Microsoft.Quantum.Intrinsic;
    open Microsoft.Quantum.Canon;

    operation CreateSuperposition() : Result[] {
        using (qubits = Qubit[2]) {
```

```
        H(qubits[0]); // Apply Hadamard gate
to qubit 0
        CNOT(qubits[0], qubits[1]); // Apply
CNOT gate to entangle qubits
        return  M(qubits);  //  Measure  the
qubits
    }
  }
}
```

- **Explanation**:

  o `H(qubits[0])` creates a **superposition** of the first qubit.

  o `CNOT(qubits[0],  qubits[1])` creates **entanglement** between the two qubits.

  o `M(qubits)` measures the state of the qubits and returns the results.

20.2 How Quantum Computing Affects Python and C# Applications

As quantum computing progresses, developers will need to consider how quantum capabilities can be integrated into classical software applications. Both **Python** and **C#** are already adapting to quantum computing technologies, allowing developers to take advantage of quantum capabilities while maintaining compatibility with classical systems.

1. Quantum Computing and Python

Python is widely used in the **quantum computing** ecosystem because it has an extensive set of libraries and tools for working with quantum algorithms. **Qiskit**, developed by **IBM**, is a popular Python library for quantum computing, providing tools to simulate quantum circuits and run algorithms on quantum hardware.

- **Integrating Python with Quantum Computing**:
    - **Qiskit** allows you to create, simulate, and run quantum circuits on IBM's **quantum hardware**.
    - Python's role in quantum computing is typically focused on the **classical control** of quantum algorithms, such as data analysis and communication with quantum simulators.
- **Example: Running a Quantum Algorithm with Qiskit**:

```python
python
```

275

```python
from qiskit import QuantumCircuit,
execute, Aer

# Create a quantum circuit with one qubit
qc = QuantumCircuit(1, 1)

# Apply a Hadamard gate to the qubit
qc.h(0)

# Measure the qubit
qc.measure(0, 0)

# Simulate the quantum circuit
simulator =
Aer.get_backend('qasm_simulator')
result = execute(qc, simulator,
shots=1000).result()

# Print the result
counts = result.get_counts()
print(counts)
```

- **Explanation**:
  - o **QuantumCircuit(1, 1)** creates a quantum circuit with one qubit and one classical bit.
  - o The **Hadamard gate** creates a superposition.
  - o The **measure** function measures the qubit's state.

o **Aerospace backend** is used for simulation.

2. Quantum Computing and C#

C# integrates well with quantum computing through **Microsoft's Quantum Development Kit (QDK)**, which includes **Q#** for writing quantum algorithms and **.NET** libraries for managing classical components. C# is used for controlling and interacting with quantum operations written in **Q#**.

- **Interfacing Quantum Computing with C#**:
    - o Developers can use C# to **manage the quantum application** and execute Q# operations in the context of a larger classical application.
    - o **Quantum simulators** like the **Quantum Simulator** in the QDK can be used to run quantum algorithms within the **.NET environment**.
- **Example: Calling Q# from C#**:

```csharp

using
Microsoft.Quantum.Simulation.Simulators;
using Microsoft.Quantum.Calls;
using System;
```

```csharp
class Program
{
    static void Main(string[] args)
    {
        using (var qsim = new QuantumSimulator())
        {
            var result = CreateSuperposition.Run(qsim).Result;

            Console.WriteLine("Measurement results: ");
            foreach (var r in result)
            {
                Console.WriteLine(r);
            }
        }
    }
}
```

- **Explanation**:
  - This C# code calls a quantum operation (CreateSuperposition) from a quantum simulator.
  - The results are printed to the console after executing the quantum operation in the simulation.

278

20.3 Future Trends in Hybrid Cloud and Quantum Computing

As quantum computing technology continues to evolve, **hybrid cloud** systems—where classical and quantum computing coexist—will become increasingly important. The cloud will provide the **scalable infrastructure** necessary for quantum computers to function effectively, making quantum computing more accessible to businesses and developers.

1. Hybrid Cloud Models

- **Quantum Cloud**: Quantum computers require specific hardware, and traditional cloud infrastructure (like **AWS**, **Azure**, or **Google Cloud**) will provide the necessary resources to run quantum algorithms via **quantum-as-a-service** (QaaS). This enables developers to access quantum hardware on demand.

- **Classical and Quantum Integration**: Quantum algorithms will often need to be integrated with classical processing. This requires **hybrid systems**

279

that combine **quantum and classical computing** to solve complex problems. Developers can use quantum computing for specialized tasks, such as optimization or cryptography, while relying on classical computers for other processing.

- **Quantum Cloud Services**: Cloud providers like **Microsoft Azure Quantum**, **IBM Q**, and **Amazon Braket** offer platforms to run quantum algorithms in the cloud, allowing seamless integration between quantum and classical systems.

2. Quantum Cryptography and Security

Quantum computing poses a potential threat to classical cryptographic systems, particularly those based on **RSA** and **ECC**. As quantum computers become more powerful, they will be able to break these encryption systems by efficiently solving the **factoring problem** and the **discrete logarithm problem**.

- **Post-Quantum Cryptography**: In response, researchers are developing new cryptographic algorithms designed to be secure against quantum attacks. This is a growing area of research and will play a vital role in the **future of data security**.

Conclusion

In this chapter, we explored how **quantum computing** is shaping the future of programming. We introduced **Q#** as a language for quantum programming, demonstrated how quantum computing could affect **Python** and **C#** applications, and discussed the **hybrid cloud** approach to integrating quantum and classical computing. As quantum technology continues to mature, it will transform areas such as **optimization**, **cryptography**, and **AI**, unlocking new possibilities for developers and businesses.

The future of programming is inevitably linked with **quantum computing**, and understanding how to work with this new paradigm will be crucial for tomorrow's developers.

In the next chapter, we will dive into **quantum algorithms** and explore their applications in **real-world scenarios**.

Let's continue building! 🚀

Part 8

Practical Case Studies and Career Growth

Chapter 21

Migrating Legacy Applications to Modern Frameworks

Migrating **legacy applications** to **modern frameworks** is a critical task for many organizations seeking to stay competitive in an ever-evolving tech landscape. This process often involves refactoring outdated code, re-architecting systems, and embracing cloud technologies to take advantage of scalability, flexibility, and performance improvements. In this chapter, we will explore how to **refactor old applications for the cloud**, dive into a **real-world case study** of **modernizing a legacy C# application**, and discuss the **performance trade-offs** and **migration best practices** that developers must consider during the process.

21.1 How to Refactor Old Applications for the Cloud

The transition from **legacy on-premises systems** to **cloud-native architectures** involves several steps. These steps vary based on the complexity of the legacy system and the target cloud platform, but generally, they involve:

1. Assessment and Planning

Before you begin the migration process, you need to assess the current state of your legacy application and define a clear plan for how to modernize it.

- **Application Inventory**: Identify all the components of the legacy application, including code, databases, third-party dependencies, and user interfaces.
- **Cloud Readiness**: Assess whether the legacy application can be lifted-and-shifted directly to the cloud or if it requires **re-architecture**. For instance, some legacy applications may need to be refactored for better scalability and performance in cloud environments.

2. Choosing the Right Cloud Platform and Architecture

Once the assessment is complete, the next step is to choose a cloud provider and the appropriate **cloud architecture** for the application.

- **IaaS (Infrastructure as a Service)**: If the application cannot be easily refactored, it might make sense to run it in a **virtual machine** on the cloud (lift-and-shift).
- **PaaS (Platform as a Service)**: If possible, refactor the application to take advantage of **managed cloud services** such as **Azure App Service, AWS Elastic Beanstalk**, or **Google App Engine**.
- **Serverless**: If your application can be broken down into discrete functions, consider **serverless computing** with platforms like **AWS Lambda** or **Azure Functions**.
- **Microservices**: For complex, monolithic applications, consider breaking it into **microservices** that can be independently scaled and deployed.

3. Refactoring and Replatforming

The next step is to either **refactor** (rewrite parts of the code) or **replatform** (move the application to a cloud environment with minimal code changes).

- **Refactoring** involves modifying the code to take advantage of cloud features like **auto-scaling, managed databases**, and **load balancing**.
- **Replatforming** typically involves adjusting the application to run on a cloud platform without making

significant changes to the core functionality (e.g., moving from on-premises SQL Server to **Azure SQL**).

4. Testing and Validation

Once the migration has been completed, testing becomes crucial to ensure that the application performs as expected in the cloud. Key areas to test include:

- **Performance and Scalability**: Does the cloud environment scale properly to handle peak loads?
- **Security**: Are all security protocols in place for data encryption, access control, and identity management?
- **Functionality**: Does the migrated application meet all the business requirements without regressions?

21.2 Case Study: Modernizing a Legacy C# Application

Let's take a real-world example of modernizing a **legacy C# application**. Imagine that you are working for a financial services company that has a legacy C# application running on **Windows Server** and using **SQL Server** for storage.

This application was developed over 10 years ago and is becoming increasingly difficult to maintain and scale.

1. Initial Assessment

- The application is a monolithic **C# desktop application** that communicates with a **SQL Server** database.
- It lacks modern features like **cloud integration**, **web-based interfaces**, and **mobile compatibility**.
- The application is not optimized for **cloud-scale** and requires significant hardware resources to handle peak demand.

2. Deciding on the Cloud Strategy

After assessing the application, the following decisions were made:

- **Replatforming to Azure**: Rather than rewriting the application, the decision was made to replatform it to **Azure App Service** for easier management and auto-scaling.
- **SQL Server to Azure SQL**: The **SQL Server** database will be migrated to **Azure SQL Database**, taking advantage of the platform's scalability and managed backup services.

- **Web-based Frontend**: The old desktop UI will be replaced with a **web-based interface** using **ASP.NET Core** to make it accessible from anywhere.

3. The Refactoring Process

The migration and refactoring process took place in phases:

- **Phase 1: Database Migration**:
  - The first step was to migrate the database from **SQL Server** to **Azure SQL Database**.
  - Data migration was done using **Azure Database Migration Service** to ensure no data loss.
  - Stored procedures were refactored to utilize **Azure SQL's scaling capabilities**.
- **Phase 2: Application Migration**:
  - The core C# application was refactored to run on **Azure App Service**, leveraging the **App Service plan** to automatically scale with usage.
  - The old desktop UI was replaced with a **responsive web application** using **ASP.NET Core** for a modern, cross-platform experience.
- **Phase 3: Integrating with Cloud Services**:
  - The application was integrated with **Azure Blob Storage** for document management and **Azure Active Directory** for user authentication.

- o The application was refactored to use **Azure Key Vault** for secure management of sensitive credentials and API keys.

4. Deployment and Testing

After refactoring, the application was deployed to **Azure App Service** and thoroughly tested:

- **Performance Testing**: Ensured the application could handle thousands of concurrent users, taking advantage of Azure's **auto-scaling** and **load balancing**.
- **User Acceptance Testing**: Ensured the user experience was consistent with the old desktop application, while also taking advantage of the new web-based UI.
- **Security Testing**: Verified that **Azure Security Center** provided the necessary security measures and that all data in transit was **encrypted**.

5. Final Outcome

After successfully migrating the legacy C# application to the cloud:

- The application became more scalable, reliable, and cost-effective by using **Azure App Service** and **Azure SQL Database**.

- The new **web-based interface** increased accessibility and reduced the need for desktop installations.
- The company experienced **faster deployment cycles** and better security controls with **Azure Active Directory** and **Key Vault**.

21.3 Performance Trade-Offs and Migration Best Practices

While migrating legacy applications to modern frameworks offers numerous benefits, there are several **performance trade-offs** and best practices to consider during the migration process.

1. Performance Trade-Offs

- **Latency**: Moving applications from on-premises to the cloud may introduce network latency, particularly if the cloud region is far from the user base. This can be mitigated by choosing cloud regions close to end-users.
- **Data Transfer Costs**: Migrating large databases or applications to the cloud can incur significant data transfer costs, especially if the migration process

involves transferring large amounts of data between on-premises and cloud environments. Use **Azure Data Box** or **AWS Snowball** for bulk data transfers.

- **Dependency on Internet Connectivity**: Cloud applications are dependent on **internet connectivity**, which can affect availability and performance in case of outages. Implementing **offline capabilities** or **local caches** can help mitigate this issue.

2. Best Practices for Migration

- **Incremental Migration**: Migrate parts of the application incrementally to ensure minimal disruption. This could involve starting with non-critical components or using **hybrid cloud solutions** to connect the on-premises infrastructure with the cloud.
- **Automation**: Automate the migration process with tools like **Azure Migrate** or **AWS Migration Hub** to reduce manual effort and minimize errors.
- **Security**: Pay attention to security during the migration. Use **encryption** for data in transit, and ensure that the new cloud infrastructure is configured according to best practices (e.g., using **security groups** and **firewalls**).
- **Monitoring and Optimization**: After migration, continuously monitor the application with tools like

291

Azure Monitor, **AWS CloudWatch**, or **Google Stackdriver** to optimize performance and scalability.

Conclusion

Migrating legacy applications to modern frameworks and cloud platforms offers significant benefits, including improved scalability, performance, and security. In this chapter, we explored how to **refactor old applications for the cloud**, used a **real-world case study** of modernizing a **C# legacy application**, and discussed the **performance trade-offs** and **migration best practices** to ensure a smooth transition.

As businesses continue to embrace cloud-native technologies, mastering the process of modernizing legacy applications will be an essential skill for developers and architects alike.

In the next chapter, we will explore **career growth** and the essential skills needed to thrive in the rapidly changing world of software development.

Let's continue building! 🚀

Chapter 22

Full-Stack Development with Python and C#

Full-stack development refers to the practice of working with both the **front-end** and **back-end** of a web application. While **Python** is commonly used for **back-end** development, **C#** is a powerful language for **front-end** development, particularly with frameworks like **Blazor** and **ASP.NET Core**. In this chapter, we will explore how to **combine a Python back-end with a C# front-end**, develop a **cloud-based collaboration tool**, and discuss **deployment strategies** for full-stack applications.

22.1 How to Combine Python Backend with C# Frontend

Combining a Python-based backend with a C# frontend is an interesting challenge that requires both **interoperability** and **integration**. A Python back-end (using frameworks like

Flask or **Django**) can handle the application logic, API, and database interactions, while the C# front-end (using **Blazor** or **ASP.NET Core MVC**) handles user interfaces and client-side interactions.

1. Backend with Python (Flask/Django)

- **Python frameworks like Flask and Django** are ideal for handling the backend of your application. Flask is lightweight and simple, while Django provides a more extensive set of tools for building complex applications.
- The backend typically exposes **RESTful APIs** (or **GraphQL**) that the frontend can interact with via HTTP requests.

2. Frontend with C# (Blazor/ASP.NET Core)

- **Blazor** is a modern framework from **Microsoft** that allows you to build interactive web UIs using **C#** instead of JavaScript. Blazor can run on the server (Blazor Server) or in the browser via WebAssembly (Blazor WebAssembly).
- **ASP.NET Core MVC** is a popular C# framework for building web applications with **Model-View-Controller** architecture.

294

3. Communication Between Python and C#

To connect the Python backend and C# frontend, the most common approach is to use **HTTP requests** (via **AJAX** or **Fetch** in the front-end), where the front-end sends HTTP requests to the Python back-end, which processes the request and returns data.

- **Backend in Python (Flask Example)**: Here's how you might create a simple **Flask API** that handles user authentication and returns a response:

python

```
from flask import Flask, jsonify, request
app = Flask(__name__)

@app.route('/api/auth', methods=['POST'])
def authenticate_user():
    data = request.json
    if data['username'] == 'admin' and
data['password'] == 'password123':
        return            jsonify({"status":
"success",          "message":          "User
authenticated"})
    else:
```

```
        return            jsonify({"status":
"failure",        "message":       "Invalid
credentials"}), 401


if __name__ == '__main__':
    app.run(debug=True)
```

- **Frontend in C# (Blazor Example)**: Here's a simple **Blazor WebAssembly** component that makes a POST request to the **Flask backend** to authenticate a user:

```csharp
@page "/login"
@inject HttpClient Http

<h3>Login</h3>

<input     type="text"     @bind="username"
placeholder="Username" />
<input    type="password"  @bind="password"
placeholder="Password" />
<button
@onclick="AuthenticateUser">Login</button
>

@code {
    private string username;
```

```csharp
private string password;

private async Task AuthenticateUser()
{
    var loginData = new { username,
password };
    var response = await
Http.PostAsJsonAsync("https://localhost:5
000/api/auth", loginData);

    if (response.IsSuccessStatusCode)
    {
        var result = await
response.Content.ReadFromJsonAsync<Dictio
nary<string, string>>();

Console.WriteLine(result["message"]);
    }
    else
    {

Console.WriteLine("Authentication
failed!");
    }
}
}
```

- **Explanation**:

- o The **Flask backend** exposes an `/api/auth` endpoint to authenticate users.

- o The **Blazor front-end** sends an HTTP POST request with the username and password.

- o The front-end processes the response and either shows a success message or failure, depending on the authentication result.

22.2 Real-World Example: Developing a Cloud-Based Collaboration Tool

Let's build a **cloud-based collaboration tool** with a **Python backend** and a **C# frontend** using the **Blazor framework** for real-time collaboration on documents or tasks. This example will include:

- **User Authentication**: Managed by the Python backend with **Flask**.

- **Real-Time Updates**: Handled using **SignalR** (via Blazor for the C# front-end).

- **Cloud Storage**: Documents and files are stored in the cloud (e.g., **Azure Blob Storage**).

1. Backend (Flask + Azure Storage)

In this example, the **Flask backend** will handle user authentication, document uploads, and storage using **Azure Blob Storage**.

- **Install Azure Blob Storage SDK**:

```bash
bash

pip install azure-storage-blob
```

- **Flask Backend Code (File Upload)**:

```python
python

from flask import Flask, request, jsonify
from      azure.storage.blob      import
BlobServiceClient

app = Flask(__name__)
connection_string = 'your-azure-storage-
connection-string'
blob_service_client                      =
BlobServiceClient.from_connection_string(
connection_string)
container_name = "collaboration-container"

@app.route('/upload', methods=['POST'])
```

299

```python
def upload_file():
    file = request.files['file']
    blob_client                        =
blob_service_client.get_blob_client(conta
iner=container_name, blob=file.filename)
    blob_client.upload_blob(file)
    return jsonify({"status": "success",
"message": "File uploaded successfully!"})


if __name__ == '__main__':
    app.run(debug=True)
```

2. Frontend (Blazor + SignalR)

The **Blazor front-end** will allow real-time collaboration by integrating **SignalR**, which enables bi-directional communication between the client and server.

- **Install SignalR Client in Blazor**: Add the **Microsoft.AspNetCore.SignalR.Client** NuGet package to the Blazor project.
- **Blazor Code for Real-Time Collaboration**: Here's a Blazor component for real-time updates and file uploads:

```csharp
@page "/collaborate"
@inject HttpClient Http
```

300

```
@using Microsoft.AspNetCore.SignalR.Client

<h3>Collaborate on Document</h3>

<input type="file" @onchange="UploadFile"
/>
<button
@onclick="StartCollaboration">Start
Collaboration</button>

<ul id="messagesList">
    @foreach (var message in messages)
    {
        <li>@message</li>
    }
</ul>

@code {
    private HubConnection? hubConnection;
    private List<string> messages = new
List<string>();

    protected override async Task
OnInitializedAsync()
    {
        hubConnection          =          new
HubConnectionBuilder()

.WithUrl("https://localhost:5000/hub")
```

```
                    .Build();


hubConnection.On<string>("ReceiveMessage"
, (message) =>
        {
            messages.Add(message);
            InvokeAsync(StateHasChanged);
        });


        await hubConnection.StartAsync();
    }


    private          async          Task
StartCollaboration()
    {
        await
hubConnection.SendAsync("SendMessage",
"User    has    joined    the    document
collaboration.");
    }


    private          async          Task
UploadFile(ChangeEventArgs e)
    {
        var file = e.Value.ToString();
        var      content      =      new
MultipartFormDataContent();
```

```
        content.Add(new
StringContent(file), "file");

        var    response    =    await
Http.PostAsync("https://localhost:5000/up
load", content);
        if (response.IsSuccessStatusCode)
        {
            await
hubConnection.SendAsync("SendMessage",
"New file uploaded to the collaboration
document.");
        }
    }
}
```

- **Explanation**:
  - The Blazor front-end uses **SignalR** to send real-time messages to all connected clients, allowing users to see updates as other users join the document or upload files.
  - The file is uploaded to the **Flask backend**, which stores it in **Azure Blob Storage**.

22.3 Deployment Strategies for Full-Stack Applications

When deploying a **full-stack Python and C# application**, several strategies need to be considered to ensure the application is scalable, secure, and maintainable.

1. Hosting the Backend (Python)

- **Cloud Providers**: The Python backend can be hosted on services like **Azure App Service, AWS Elastic Beanstalk**, or **Google App Engine.**

- **Containerization**: Use **Docker** to containerize the backend and deploy it to **Kubernetes** for scaling and management.

- **Serverless**: If the Python backend can be divided into stateless functions, consider using **Azure Functions** or **AWS Lambda** for a serverless deployment.

2. Hosting the Frontend (C# with Blazor)

- **Blazor WebAssembly**: If using Blazor WebAssembly, the app can be deployed to a static site hosting service like **Azure Static Web Apps, Netlify**, or **AWS S3**.

- **Blazor Server**: For Blazor Server, use **Azure App Service** or **AWS Elastic Beanstalk** to host the app, ensuring real-time communication with **SignalR**.

3. Database and Storage

- Use **Azure SQL Database, Amazon RDS**, or **Google Cloud SQL** for relational databases.
- For **file storage**, use **Azure Blob Storage, Amazon S3**, or **Google Cloud Storage** to store documents, images, or other media.

4. Continuous Integration/Continuous Deployment (CI/CD)

- **CI/CD Tools**: Use **GitHub Actions, Azure DevOps**, or **Jenkins** to automate testing, building, and deployment processes for both the frontend and backend.

Conclusion

In this chapter, we explored how to combine a **Python backend** with a **C# frontend** to build a **full-stack application**. We discussed the integration of **Flask** and **Blazor**, creating a **cloud-based collaboration tool** that allows real-time collaboration and document management. Additionally, we examined **deployment strategies** for full-stack applications, including cloud hosting, containerization, and serverless approaches.

By mastering full-stack development with Python and C#, developers can build highly scalable and maintainable applications that leverage the strengths of both languages.

In the next chapter, we will explore **advanced deployment strategies** and **performance optimizations** to take your applications to the next level.

Let's continue building! 🚀

Chapter 23

IoT and Embedded Systems with Python and C#

The **Internet of Things (IoT)** and **embedded systems** have become essential components of modern technology. With devices being interconnected and able to exchange data, IoT has a wide range of applications, from **smart homes** and **industrial automation** to **healthcare** and **agriculture**. In this chapter, we will explore how to build IoT applications using **Python** and **C#** with platforms like **Raspberry Pi** and **Azure IoT Hub**. Additionally, we will walk through a **hands-on project** to create a **smart home automation system** and address the **security challenges** involved in IoT development.

23.1 Building IoT Applications with Raspberry Pi and Azure IoT Hub

The **Raspberry Pi** is one of the most popular platforms for building IoT applications due to its low cost, accessibility, and wide support for **Python** and **C#** programming. Coupled with **Azure IoT Hub**, Microsoft's fully managed IoT service, it allows developers to easily connect, monitor, and manage IoT devices.

1. Raspberry Pi for IoT Development

The **Raspberry Pi** is a small, affordable computer that supports various sensors, actuators, and wireless communication protocols (like **Wi-Fi** and **Bluetooth**). It is highly versatile and can run a full operating system (usually **Raspberry Pi OS**, a Debian-based Linux distribution), which makes it ideal for building IoT prototypes.

- **Getting Started with Raspberry Pi**:
  - Install **Raspberry Pi OS** on a microSD card.
  - Set up **SSH** or connect a **keyboard** and **monitor** to interact with the device.
  - Install libraries such as **RPi.GPIO** (for general-purpose input/output pins) or **Adafruit_IO** (for cloud IoT integration).

2. Azure IoT Hub for Cloud Integration

Azure IoT Hub is a cloud service from Microsoft designed for managing and securely communicating with IoT devices. It allows for **bi-directional communication** between IoT devices and cloud-based applications.

- **Setting Up Azure IoT Hub**:
    1. **Create an IoT Hub** in the **Azure Portal**.
    2. **Register** your device (e.g., Raspberry Pi) in the IoT Hub to obtain the **device connection string**.
    3. Use the **Azure IoT SDKs** to connect the Raspberry Pi to the IoT Hub.

3. Python IoT Development on Raspberry Pi

Python is one of the most commonly used languages for IoT development due to its simplicity and support for various libraries. Here's an example of how you can connect a Raspberry Pi to **Azure IoT Hub** using **Python**.

- **Install the Azure IoT SDK for Python**:

```bash
bash
```

```bash
pip install azure-iot-device
```

- **Python Example to Send Telemetry Data to Azure IoT Hub**:

```python
from azure.iot.device import
IoTHubDeviceClient, Message
import time

CONNECTION_STRING = "<Your IoT Hub device
connection string>"
client =
IoTHubDeviceClient.create_from_connection
_string(CONNECTION_STRING)

def send_telemetry_data():
    while True:
        telemetry_data = '{"temperature":
22.5, "humidity": 60}'
        message = Message(telemetry_data)
        client.send_message(message)
        print(f"Sent telemetry data:
{telemetry_data}")
        time.sleep(5)

send_telemetry_data()
```

- **Explanation**:

- This code connects the Raspberry Pi to the Azure IoT Hub and sends telemetry data (temperature and humidity) in JSON format.
- The **IoTHubDeviceClient** object facilitates communication between the Raspberry Pi and IoT Hub.
- This telemetry data can then be processed or visualized in Azure services such as **Azure Stream Analytics** or **Power BI**.

4. C# IoT Development on Raspberry Pi

While Python is popular for IoT development on Raspberry Pi, **C#** is also supported, especially through the **.NET IoT** libraries.

- **Install .NET IoT SDK**:

```bash
dotnet add package System.Device.Gpio
dotnet add package Microsoft.Azure.Devices.Client
```

- **C# Example to Connect Raspberry Pi to Azure IoT Hub**:

311

```csharp
using Microsoft.Azure.Devices.Client;
using System;
using System.Text;
using System.Threading.Tasks;

class Program
{
    static async Task Main(string[] args)
    {
        var connectionString = "<Your IoT Hub device connection string>";
        var deviceClient = DeviceClient.CreateFromConnectionString(connectionString, TransportType.Mqtt);

        while (true)
        {
            var telemetryData = "{ \"temperature\": 22.5, \"humidity\": 60 }";
            var message = new Message(Encoding.ASCII.GetBytes(telemetryData));
            await deviceClient.SendEventAsync(message);
            Console.WriteLine($"Sent: {telemetryData}");
```

```
                    await Task.Delay(5000);
        }
    }
}
```

- **Explanation**:
  - This C# code uses the **Microsoft.Azure.Devices.Client** package to send telemetry data from Raspberry Pi to Azure IoT Hub.

23.2 Hands-On Project: Creating a Smart Home Automation System

In this section, we will create a **smart home automation system** that controls a light bulb based on temperature and motion sensors, and interacts with **Azure IoT Hub** for data analytics and cloud control.

1. Components Needed

- **Raspberry Pi** (with Raspberry Pi OS installed)
- **DHT22 sensor** (for temperature and humidity)
- **PIR motion sensor** (to detect motion)

- **Relay module** (to control a light bulb)
- **Azure IoT Hub** for cloud connectivity

2. Wiring the Components

- Connect the **DHT22 sensor** to the Raspberry Pi's GPIO pins to read temperature and humidity.
- Connect the **PIR motion sensor** to detect motion in the room.
- Use a **relay module** to control the on/off state of a light bulb.

3. Python Code for IoT Device Interaction

The following Python code reads data from the **DHT22** and **PIR** sensors, sends telemetry data to **Azure IoT Hub**, and controls the light based on motion detection.

```python
python

import RPi.GPIO as GPIO
from azure.iot.device import IoTHubDeviceClient,
Message
import time
import Adafruit_DHT

# Setup for GPIO
GPIO.setmode(GPIO.BCM)
```

```python
GPIO.setup(18, GPIO.OUT)  # Relay to control the
light (GPIO pin 18)


# Setup for DHT22 (temperature and humidity
sensor)
sensor = Adafruit_DHT.DHT22
pin = 4  # GPIO pin where the DHT22 is connected

# Azure IoT Hub connection string
CONNECTION_STRING = "<Your IoT Hub device
connection string>"
client                                        =
IoTHubDeviceClient.create_from_connection_strin
g(CONNECTION_STRING)

def send_telemetry_data(temperature, humidity):
    telemetry_data      =      f'{{"temperature":
{temperature}, "humidity": {humidity}}}'
    message = Message(telemetry_data)
    client.send_message(message)
    print(f"Sent data: {telemetry_data}")

def monitor_motion():
    try:
        while True:
            # Get temperature and humidity from
DHT22 sensor
            humidity,         temperature        =
Adafruit_DHT.read_retry(sensor, pin)
```

315

```
        if  humidity  is  not  None  and
temperature is not None:

send_telemetry_data(temperature, humidity)

        #  Read  PIR  sensor  for  motion
detection
        if  GPIO.input(17):    #  PIR  sensor
connected to GPIO pin 17
            print("Motion detected!")
            GPIO.output(18,  GPIO.HIGH)    #
Turn on the light
        else:
            GPIO.output(18,  GPIO.LOW)    #
Turn off the light

        time.sleep(5)

    except KeyboardInterrupt:
        print("Exiting...")
        GPIO.cleanup()

monitor_motion()
```

- **Explanation**:
  - o The **DHT22** sensor reads the temperature and humidity, and this data is sent to **Azure IoT Hub**.

o The **PIR motion sensor** detects motion in the room, and when motion is detected, the relay is activated to turn on the light.

o The system continuously monitors sensor data and sends it to the cloud every 5 seconds.

23.3 Security Challenges in IoT Development

As IoT applications become more widespread, security remains a critical challenge. IoT devices often collect and transmit sensitive data, making them attractive targets for hackers. Ensuring **data security**, **device integrity**, and **network safety** is vital for IoT development.

1. Device Security

IoT devices like the Raspberry Pi can be vulnerable to **unauthorized access**. It is essential to:

- **Use secure boot mechanisms** to prevent unauthorized firmware.

317

- **Encrypt device communications** using **TLS/SSL** to protect data in transit.
- **Regularly update device firmware** to patch known vulnerabilities.

2. Authentication and Authorization

Proper authentication mechanisms must be in place to ensure that only authorized devices and users can interact with the IoT system.

- **Use strong passwords** and **multi-factor authentication (MFA)** for device management.
- **JWT (JSON Web Tokens)** and **OAuth** can be used for secure API authentication.

3. Data Security and Privacy

IoT devices collect vast amounts of data, often sensitive, such as location, personal habits, and health information.

- **Encrypt sensitive data** both at rest and in transit.
- Use cloud-based security features, such as **Azure IoT Hub's device authentication** and **role-based access control (RBAC)**.

4. Network Security

IoT networks often involve a large number of devices, each representing a potential point of vulnerability.

- Use **VPNs** or **private networks** to isolate IoT devices from the open internet.
- Implement **firewalls** and **intrusion detection systems** to monitor for malicious activity.

Conclusion

In this chapter, we explored how to build **IoT applications** with **Python** and **C#**, focusing on integrating **Raspberry Pi** with **Azure IoT Hub** for cloud connectivity. We developed a **smart home automation system** and discussed key **security challenges** in IoT development. As IoT continues to grow, ensuring security, scalability, and reliability will be essential for building robust applications.

In the next chapter, we will delve into **advanced IoT applications** and explore how emerging technologies like **edge computing** are enhancing the capabilities of IoT systems.

Part 9

The Future of Programming Careers

Chapter 24

Open Source Contributions and Community Engagement

As the tech industry evolves, developers who engage with open-source projects and participate in developer communities are not only improving their technical skills but also building strong professional networks and enhancing their careers. **Open source contributions** allow developers to collaborate with others, learn from peers, and create projects that have a tangible impact. In this chapter, we will explore why contributing to open-source projects is crucial for your career growth, how to find and contribute to **Python** and **.NET open-source communities**, and how to showcase your work on **GitHub** and **Stack Overflow**.

24.1 Why Contributing to Open-Source Projects Boosts Your Career

Contributing to open-source projects provides numerous benefits that help accelerate your career. Here are some key reasons why engaging with the open-source community is vital for developers:

1. Building a Strong Portfolio

- **Real-world experience**: Open-source contributions allow you to work on actual projects that solve real problems. By contributing, you demonstrate your ability to work in a team, write clean code, and contribute to meaningful projects.
- **Showcase your skills**: A strong open-source portfolio on platforms like **GitHub** showcases your coding skills, problem-solving abilities, and commitment to continuous learning.

2. Networking and Community Engagement

- **Connecting with other developers**: Contributing to open-source projects exposes you to a network of talented developers. It allows you to engage in discussions, learn from others, and even find potential mentors or collaborators.
- **Reputation building**: As you make valuable contributions to open-source projects, your reputation as a **trusted**

developer grows. This can lead to job offers, speaking opportunities, and invitations to collaborate on high-profile projects.

3. Enhancing Career Opportunities

- **Visibility to employers**: Many employers look at open-source contributions as a valuable sign of a developer's initiative, problem-solving skills, and willingness to learn. Active contributors to reputable projects are often noticed by hiring managers and recruiters.
- **Job prospects**: Contributing to open-source projects can make you more attractive to companies that value community engagement. It is often seen as evidence of your passion for programming and the tech community.

4. Learning and Improving Skills

- **Exposure to diverse codebases**: Working on open-source projects allows you to explore code written by other developers, exposing you to new technologies, best practices, and development methodologies.
- **Mentorship and feedback**: Open-source contributions often come with feedback from other experienced developers. This process helps you **grow** and **improve** your coding skills by learning from others' experiences.

24.2 Finding and Contributing to Python and .NET Open-Source Communities

There are vibrant open-source communities for both **Python** and **.NET**, with many projects to choose from. Whether you're a Python enthusiast or a C# developer, you can easily get involved in these communities and start contributing.

1. Finding Open-Source Projects to Contribute to

- **GitHub** is the primary platform for open-source development, where most projects are hosted. By searching for **Python** or **.NET** repositories, you can find projects that are actively seeking contributors.
    - **Search filters**: GitHub offers search filters like **"good first issue"** to help new contributors find beginner-friendly issues.
    - **Explore trending repositories**: GitHub's **Explore** section lets you find trending projects in various categories, including Python and .NET.
- **Other Platforms**:

- **GitLab**: Another platform that hosts a variety of open-source projects, with similar features to GitHub.

- **Stack Overflow**: Many open-source projects post challenges or questions on **Stack Overflow**, giving developers the opportunity to engage.

- **Contributing to Python Open-Source**:

  - The **Python Software Foundation (PSF)** supports many open-source Python projects. Look for projects such as **Django**, **Flask**, and **PyTorch** to contribute to.

  - Visit https://www.python.org/community/ to find more information about Python community-driven projects.

- **Contributing to .NET Open-Source**:

  - The **.NET Foundation** supports open-source projects for .NET developers. Projects like **ASP.NET Core**, **Entity Framework Core**, and **Xamarin** are popular places to contribute.

  - Visit **https://dotnetfoundation.org/projects** for a list of **.NET open-source** projects that welcome contributions.

2. How to Contribute

- **Fork the repository**: The first step is to **fork** the repository you want to contribute to, which creates a of the project under your account.

- **Clone the repository**: Use **git clone** to download the project to your local machine.

- **Create a new branch**: Work on your changes in a separate branch to keep the main branch clean.

- **Make your changes**: Implement your bug fixes, features, or improvements.

- **Create a pull request**: Once your changes are complete, submit a pull request (PR) to propose your changes to the main repository.

- **Communicate and collaborate**: Engage with project maintainers and other contributors to review your pull request and iterate based on their feedback.

24.3 How to Showcase Your Projects on GitHub and Stack Overflow

1. Showcasing Projects on GitHub

- **Create a well-documented repository**: Make sure your repository has a clear **README** file that explains the purpose of the project, how to install and use it, and how to contribute.
- **Add descriptive commit messages**: Use clear, concise commit messages that explain what changes were made and why.
- **Include a license**: Choose an appropriate open-source license for your project (e.g., MIT, Apache 2.0, GPL).
- **Tag releases**: When your project reaches significant milestones, create tags or **releases** to mark them, making it easy for others to follow the progress.

Example of a well-documented **README** file:

```markdown
# My Awesome Python Project

## Description
This project is a Python-based web scraper that
collects data from various sources.

## Features
- Scrapes multiple websites
```

- Saves data in a CSV file
- Sends email notifications on success

Installation
Clone this repository:
```bash
git                                     clone
https://github.com/yourusername/awesome-python-
project.git
cd awesome-python-project
pip install -r requirements.txt
```

Usage

Run the script:

```bash

python scraper.py
```

Contributing

1. Fork the repository
2. Create a feature branch (`git checkout -b feature-branch`)
3. Commit your changes (`git commit -am 'Add new feature'`)

4. **Push to the branch** (`git push origin feature-branch`)

5. **Open a pull request**

```markdown
```

2. How to Build a Strong Stack Overflow Profile

- **Answer questions**: Engage with the community by answering questions related to your areas of expertise. Ensure your answers are clear, detailed, and backed by examples or code snippets.
- **Ask well-researched questions**: When you encounter an issue, ask clear and specific questions. Provide relevant details, including error messages, steps to reproduce, and what you've tried already.
- **Contribute to tags**: Add relevant tags to your questions and answers to help others find the content more easily.
- **Build a reputation**: As you provide helpful answers and contribute to discussions, you'll gain **upvotes** and **reputation points**, which will increase your visibility and credibility in the community.

24.4 The Power of Open Source in Career Development

Engaging with the open-source community offers significant advantages for your career:

- **Show your expertise**: Active contributions to popular open-source projects help you demonstrate your expertise to potential employers or clients.
- **Create impact**: By contributing to important open-source projects, you can leave a tangible legacy and build a positive reputation.
- **Collaborate with global talent**: Open source allows you to work with developers from all over the world, expanding your network and learning from diverse perspectives.
- **Enhance job opportunities**: Many companies actively seek developers with open-source experience because it showcases initiative, collaboration, and technical depth.

Conclusion

Contributing to open-source projects and engaging with developer communities is a powerful way to accelerate your career. By showcasing your work on **GitHub** and **Stack Overflow**, collaborating with other developers, and making meaningful contributions to projects, you build a strong portfolio and reputation. Whether you're working with **Python**, **.NET**, or any other technology, open source provides ample opportunities to **grow your skills**, **expand your network**, and **gain career momentum**.

In the next chapter, we will explore the **future of programming careers**, looking at emerging technologies and skills that will shape the next generation of software developers.

Let's continue building! 🚀

Chapter 25

Becoming a Cross-Platform Developer

As the software development landscape continues to evolve, developers are increasingly expected to work across multiple platforms—web, mobile, cloud, and AI. Becoming a **cross-platform developer** not only makes you more versatile but also opens up a wide range of career opportunities. In this chapter, we will explore various **career paths** in cloud development, **AI**, and **mobile applications**, discuss how to **future-proof** your skills by learning **Python**, **C#**, and other technologies, and review **certifications** and **learning resources** to help you on your journey.

25.1 Career Paths in Cloud Development, AI, and Mobile Applications

The demand for skilled developers is growing across different sectors, and as a **cross-platform developer**, you can position yourself to work in cutting-edge areas like **cloud development**, **artificial intelligence (AI)**, and **mobile application development**. Let's explore each of these career paths.

1. Cloud Development

Cloud computing is revolutionizing the way applications are built, deployed, and scaled. By moving applications and services to the cloud, businesses can increase efficiency, flexibility, and scalability while reducing infrastructure costs. **Cloud developers** focus on creating, deploying, and maintaining cloud-based applications.

- **Skills Required**:
    o Proficiency in cloud platforms like **Microsoft Azure, AWS**, and **Google Cloud Platform**.
    o Familiarity with **cloud-native architecture** and **serverless computing**.
    o Experience with **containerization** tools like **Docker** and **Kubernetes**.
    o Knowledge of **CI/CD pipelines** for automation.
    o Strong understanding of **security best practices** for cloud applications.
- **Job Titles**:

- Cloud Developer
- Cloud Solutions Architect
- Cloud Engineer
- DevOps Engineer
- Site Reliability Engineer (SRE)

2. Artificial Intelligence (AI)

AI is a rapidly growing field that touches nearly every industry, from healthcare and finance to gaming and manufacturing. As an **AI developer**, you would work with algorithms, data processing, and machine learning models to build intelligent applications.

- **Skills Required**:
  - Strong knowledge of **Python** (especially libraries like **TensorFlow**, **Keras**, **PyTorch**, and **scikit-learn**).
  - Familiarity with **AI frameworks** and the ability to build and train machine learning models.
  - Proficiency in data processing and analysis, often using libraries like **NumPy**, **pandas**, and **Matplotlib**.
  - Experience with **deep learning** and **natural language processing (NLP)**.
- **Job Titles**:

- o AI Engineer
- o Machine Learning Engineer
- o Data Scientist
- o NLP Engineer
- o AI Researcher

3. Mobile Application Development

Mobile application development continues to be one of the most exciting and lucrative fields in the tech industry. With **cross-platform development frameworks** like **Flutter**, **React Native**, and **Xamarin**, developers can now build mobile applications that run on both iOS and Android using a single codebase.

- **Skills Required**:
  - o Knowledge of **mobile development frameworks** (React Native, Flutter, Xamarin).
  - o Familiarity with **native mobile development** (Swift for iOS, Kotlin/Java for Android).
  - o Experience with **mobile UI/UX design** principles.
  - o Understanding of **mobile performance optimization** and **app deployment processes**.
  - o Knowledge of **API integration** and cloud-based mobile solutions.
- **Job Titles**:

335

- ○ Mobile App Developer
- ○ iOS Developer
- ○ Android Developer
- ○ Cross-Platform Mobile Developer
- ○ Mobile Architect

25.2 Future-Proofing Your Skills: Python, C#, and Beyond

The technology landscape is constantly evolving, and to stay relevant, developers need to continuously learn and adapt. Here's how you can **future-proof** your skills by learning **Python**, **C#**, and other emerging technologies.

1. Python

Python is widely considered one of the most versatile and in-demand programming languages in the industry. It's used in **AI/ML**, **web development**, **data science**, **automation**, and **cloud computing**.

- **Why Python is Future-Proof**:

- o It's the primary language for **AI**, **machine learning**, and **data science**.
- o It's highly readable and beginner-friendly, making it ideal for new developers and rapid development cycles.
- o Python's **vast library ecosystem** supports everything from web frameworks (**Django**, **Flask**) to data analysis (**pandas**, **NumPy**).

- **Next Steps for Python**:
  - o Master libraries and frameworks like **TensorFlow** and **PyTorch** for AI development.
  - o Explore **cloud-native technologies** like **AWS Lambda** for serverless computing.

2. C#

C# is a powerful language for building a variety of applications, particularly in the **.NET ecosystem**. C# is commonly used in **web development** with **ASP.NET Core**, **mobile development** with **Xamarin**, and **game development** with **Unity**.

- **Why C# is Future-Proof**:
  - o It's **cross-platform** thanks to the **.NET Core** framework.

- It's widely used for **enterprise-level applications**, particularly in the finance, healthcare, and gaming sectors.
- **Microsoft's support** for C# ensures it will remain a key language in the tech stack for years to come.

- **Next Steps for C#:**
  - Learn **Xamarin** or **MAUI** for cross-platform mobile development.
  - Explore **Azure** for cloud development and learn how to integrate **C# applications** with cloud services.
  - Delve into **game development** with **Unity**.

3. Beyond Python and C#

While Python and C# are excellent choices, it's also important to expand your skills into other **emerging technologies**:

- **Cloud and DevOps**: Learn about **cloud-native development**, **serverless computing**, and **containerization**.
- **AI and Machine Learning**: Consider learning more about **reinforcement learning**, **deep learning**, and **NLP**.

- **Blockchain**: Explore **blockchain development** for decentralized applications and smart contract development.
- **Quantum Computing**: Start exploring **quantum programming** with **Q#**, **Python libraries**, and cloud-based quantum services like **Microsoft Azure Quantum** and **IBM Q**.

25.3 Certifications and Learning Resources

Certifications and continuous learning are essential for advancing your career and keeping your skills up-to-date. Let's explore some **certifications** and **learning resources** that can help you become a **cross-platform developer**.

1. Cloud Development Certifications

- **Microsoft Certified: Azure Fundamentals**
    - ○ Great for beginners to understand cloud concepts and core services.
- **AWS Certified Solutions Architect**

- o Designed for those who want to design cloud architectures on AWS.
- **Google Associate Cloud Engineer**
  - o A certification for engineers working with Google Cloud Platform (GCP).

2. AI and Machine Learning Certifications

- **Google Professional Machine Learning Engineer**
  - o A certification that covers the development and deployment of machine learning models.
- **IBM Data Science Professional Certificate**
  - o This certification provides foundational knowledge in data science and machine learning using Python.
- **Microsoft Certified: Azure AI Engineer Associate**
  - o For developers building AI solutions with Microsoft Azure.

3. Mobile Development Certifications

- **Google Associate Android Developer Certification**
  - o Focuses on Android app development using Java and Kotlin.
- **Apple Certified iOS Developer**

- o Certification for developers who want to specialize in iOS app development using Swift.
- **Microsoft Certified: Azure Developer Associate**
  - o This certification focuses on building cloud-based mobile and web applications using **C#** and **Azure**.

4. Learning Resources

- **FreeCodeCamp**: Offers extensive tutorials and courses on web development, including full-stack and cloud development.
- **Coursera**: Provides courses from top universities and companies, including certifications in Python, cloud technologies, and AI.
- **Udemy**: A popular platform with courses on Python, C#, mobile app development, and more.
- **Microsoft Learn**: A platform offering free learning paths for .NET, Azure, AI, and cloud technologies.
- **Pluralsight**: Offers high-quality courses on .NET, C#, cloud development, AI, and more.

5. Books and Documentation

- **"Python Crash Course"** by Eric Matthes: A hands-on introduction to Python, great for beginners.

- **"C# 9.0 in a Nutshell"** by Joseph Albahari: A comprehensive guide to C# for experienced developers.
- **"Designing Data-Intensive Applications"** by Martin Kleppmann: A deep dive into building scalable and resilient applications.

Conclusion

In this chapter, we explored how to become a **cross-platform developer** by diving into **cloud development, AI,** and **mobile applications**. We discussed how to **future-proof** your skills by mastering technologies like **Python** and **C#,** and explored key **certifications** and **learning resources** to enhance your expertise. By continuously learning and adapting to new technologies, you can position yourself as a versatile developer ready to tackle the challenges of tomorrow's tech landscape.

In the next chapter, we will dive into advanced techniques for optimizing your cross-platform development workflows.

Let's continue building! 🚀

Chapter 26

Building a Tech Startup with Python and C#

Turning your **coding skills** into a successful **business** is an exciting and rewarding journey. Whether you want to create a **Software-as-a-Service (SaaS)** product, build a mobile app, or solve a specific problem, combining your technical expertise with entrepreneurial vision can lead to great success. In this chapter, we'll explore how to **turn your coding skills into a business**, dive into a **case study** on building a **SaaS startup using Python and C#**, and discuss how to **find investors** and **launch your first product**.

26.1 How to Turn Your Coding Skills into a Business

Many developers dream of creating their own tech startup, but knowing how to translate your **coding skills** into a **viable**

business can be challenging. Here are some steps to help guide you:

1. Identifying a Market Need

The first step in building a successful tech business is to **identify a real-world problem** that your product will solve. Focus on areas where you:

- Have domain expertise.
- See inefficiencies or gaps that can be addressed with a software solution.
- Can create something unique or more efficient than existing solutions.

Common areas for tech startups include:

- **Productivity tools** (e.g., project management, time tracking).
- **Customer relationship management (CRM)** systems.
- **E-commerce solutions**.
- **Healthcare applications**.
- **Automation tools** for businesses.

2. Choosing the Right Technology Stack

When you're building a tech startup, you need to choose the right technology stack that will enable you to quickly prototype, scale, and maintain the product. Since your expertise lies in **Python** and **C#**, here are a few tools you might want to consider:

- **Backend (Python)**:
    - **Flask** or **Django** for building web APIs and backend services.
    - **Celery** for task management and background jobs.
    - **FastAPI** for high-performance RESTful APIs.
- **Frontend (C#)**:
    - **Blazor** for building interactive web UIs using C# instead of JavaScript.
    - **ASP.NET Core** for web applications and APIs.
    - **Xamarin** or **.NET MAUI** for building cross-platform mobile apps.
- **Database**:
    - **PostgreSQL** or **MySQL** for relational databases.
    - **MongoDB** for NoSQL databases.
    - **Azure Cosmos DB** for scalable cloud-native databases.

3. Building Your Minimum Viable Product (MVP)

An MVP is the simplest version of your product that solves the core problem for your target audience. The goal is to launch quickly and start gathering user feedback to iterate on your product. Keep the MVP small, focused, and inexpensive to build.

- Focus on the key features that will differentiate your product.
- Build the product with scalability in mind but don't worry about perfection at this stage.
- Use modern frameworks and cloud platforms to ensure ease of deployment and maintenance.

4. Establishing a Business Model

You need to determine how your startup will generate revenue. Common models for tech startups include:

- **SaaS (Subscription-based)**: Charge customers a monthly or annual fee to access your software.
- **Freemium**: Offer a basic version of the product for free and charge for premium features.

- **One-time Payment**: Charge a one-time fee for the product, suitable for software tools that don't require frequent updates.
- **Ad-supported**: Provide free software and monetize through ads.

26.2 Case Study: Building a SaaS Startup Using Python & C#

Let's walk through a case study of building a **SaaS startup** using **Python** for the backend and **C#** for the frontend. In this example, we will build a **task management** platform that helps businesses track and manage employee tasks in a collaborative environment.

1. Defining the Product: TaskMaster

- **Target Audience**: Small-to-medium businesses (SMBs) and startups that need a simple but powerful task management system.
- **Core Features**:
  - Task creation, editing, and tracking.

- o User roles and permissions (admin, manager, employee).
- o Task assignment and status updates.
- o Real-time notifications using **SignalR** (C#).

2. Building the MVP

- **Backend (Python)**:
  - o We will use **Django** to create a RESTful API for managing tasks and users.
  - o The application will store tasks and user data in a **PostgreSQL database**.
  - o **Celery** will be used for handling asynchronous tasks like sending email notifications and reminders.
- **Frontend (C#)**:
  - o **Blazor** will be used to build the web application's front-end, allowing us to write C# instead of JavaScript for the client-side code.
  - o **SignalR** will handle real-time updates for task statuses, notifications, and user activity.

3. Example Code for the Backend (Python with Django)

Here's how you might define a **Task model** and API endpoint using **Django REST Framework**:

```python
python

from django.db import models
from rest_framework import serializers, viewsets

class Task(models.Model):
    title = models.CharField(max_length=200)
    description = models.TextField()
    assigned_to = models.ForeignKey('auth.User',
related_name='tasks', on_delete=models.CASCADE)
    status = models.CharField(max_length=50,
default='Pending')
    created_at                              =
models.DateTimeField(auto_now_add=True)
    due_date = models.DateTimeField()

    def __str__(self):
        return self.title

class
TaskSerializer(serializers.ModelSerializer):
    class Meta:
        model = Task
        fields = ['id', 'title', 'description',
'assigned_to',      'status',      'created_at',
'due_date']

class TaskViewSet(viewsets.ModelViewSet):
    queryset = Task.objects.all()
```

349

```
serializer_class = TaskSerializer
```

This defines a simple **Task** model, serializes it, and creates a **viewset** to handle API calls.

4. Example Code for Frontend (C# with Blazor)

Here's an example of how you might implement task listing in a **Blazor** app:

csharp

```
@page "/tasks"
@inject HttpClient Http

<h3>Task List</h3>

<table class="table">
    <thead>
        <tr>
            <th>Title</th>
            <th>Description</th>
            <th>Status</th>
            <th>Due Date</th>
        </tr>
    </thead>
    <tbody>
        @foreach (var task in tasks)
        {
```

```
        <tr>
            <td>@task.Title</td>
            <td>@task.Description</td>
            <td>@task.Status</td>

<td>@task.DueDate.ToShortDateString()</td>
        </tr>
    }
  </tbody>
</table>

@code {
    private List<Task> tasks = new List<Task>();

    protected     override     async     Task
OnInitializedAsync()
    {
        tasks          =          await
Http.GetFromJsonAsync<List<Task>>("https://loca
lhost:5000/api/tasks");
    }

    public class Task
    {
        public string Title { get; set; }
        public string Description { get; set; }
        public string Status { get; set; }
        public DateTime DueDate { get; set; }
    }
```

}

This **Blazor component** makes an HTTP request to fetch tasks from the backend API and display them in a table.

26.3 Finding Investors and Launching Your First Product

Now that you have an MVP, the next step is to get **investors** and **launch your product**. Here's how to approach both:

1. Finding Investors

- **Angel Investors**: These are individuals who provide funding in exchange for equity or debt. They often prefer early-stage startups with a promising product.
    - **Pitch deck**: Create a well-crafted **pitch deck** that highlights your product, the market need, the technology stack, business model, and your team's experience.
    - **Networking**: Attend startup events, pitch competitions, and conferences where angel investors are likely to be present.

- **Venture Capitalists (VCs)**: If you're looking for larger funding, venture capitalists may be interested in your startup.

  o **Series A Funding**: Once you have product-market fit, VCs may invest in your company to help you scale.

- **Crowdfunding**: Platforms like **Kickstarter** and **Indiegogo** can help raise money from a community of supporters.

2. Launching Your First Product

- **Beta Testing**: Before launching, invite a select group of users to try the product and provide feedback. Use their feedback to fix bugs and improve usability.

- **Marketing**: Start building your product's brand and audience before launch. Utilize **social media**, **blogging**, and **email marketing** to create buzz.

- **Launch Platforms**: Use platforms like **Product Hunt**, **AppSumo**, or your own website to launch the product to a wider audience.

3. Post-Launch

- **Customer Support**: Provide top-notch customer service to keep users satisfied and gather more feedback.

- **Iterate and Improve**: Use feedback and analytics to continuously improve the product and add new features.
- **Scale**: As your user base grows, scale your infrastructure and operations to meet demand.

Conclusion

In this chapter, we explored how to turn your **coding skills** into a **business** by creating a **SaaS startup** using **Python** for the backend and **C#** for the frontend. We discussed the steps to build your MVP, find investors, and launch your first product. With the right approach to technology, business planning, and marketing, you can turn your startup idea into a thriving tech company.

In the next chapter, we will explore advanced techniques for scaling your startup and managing growth in the ever-changing tech landscape.

Let's continue building! 🚀

Chapter 27

Final Thoughts and What's Next

As technology continues to evolve at an accelerating pace, **software development** is at the heart of shaping the future of industries, businesses, and everyday life. In this final chapter, we will explore the **future of software development**, where **Python**, **C#**, and **multi-platform programming** are heading, and how you can **stay ahead** and continue learning in this ever-changing field.

27.1 The Future of Software Development

The landscape of software development is continuously evolving, driven by advancements in **cloud computing**, **artificial intelligence (AI)**, **machine learning (ML)**, **blockchain**, **edge computing**, and more. As a developer, understanding these trends and preparing for the future will allow you to build more **innovative, efficient**, and **scalable applications**.

1. Cloud-Native and Serverless Architectures

- **Cloud computing** will continue to dominate as businesses shift from traditional on-premises infrastructure to **cloud-native applications**. This means more development on platforms like **Azure, AWS**, and **Google Cloud**, as well as embracing **serverless computing**, which allows developers to build applications without worrying about managing servers.

- **Multi-cloud strategies** and **hybrid clouds** will also become more common, requiring developers to be proficient in cloud integration.

2. AI, Machine Learning, and Automation

- **AI and ML** are revolutionizing the way software is developed and used. As more companies integrate **AI-powered** features into their applications, there will be a growing need for developers to have knowledge of **machine learning algorithms, data science**, and **AI tools**.

- **Automation** in development, testing, and deployment will continue to streamline workflows, with tools like **CI/CD pipelines, automated testing**, and **infrastructure as code** becoming standard practice.

3. Edge Computing and IoT

- **Edge computing** will grow as more devices become interconnected through the **Internet of Things (IoT)**. Developers will need to create solutions that process data at the edge, closer to where it is generated, reducing latency and bandwidth usage.
- The integration of **AI with IoT** will also create new opportunities for developing intelligent systems, particularly in industries like healthcare, manufacturing, and smart cities.

4. Blockchain and Decentralized Systems

- **Blockchain technology** will continue to disrupt industries, from **finance** and **supply chain management** to **identity verification** and **smart contracts**. Developers with expertise in **blockchain** will be in high demand, especially as decentralized applications (dApps) become more common.
- The rise of **NFTs (Non-Fungible Tokens)** and **decentralized finance (DeFi)** is also opening new doors for developers to innovate.

5. Development Tools and IDEs

- **Integrated Development Environments (IDEs)** will evolve to become even more **intelligent**, integrating AI and **code suggestions** to improve productivity. **Visual Studio, PyCharm**, and other tools will continue to evolve with smarter features to assist developers in writing cleaner code, debugging faster, and reducing development time.

27.2 Where Python, C#, and Multi-Platform Programming Are Heading

As we look to the future, both **Python** and **C#** will continue to be at the forefront of **cross-platform development**. However, their roles in the development ecosystem will evolve as new technologies emerge.

1. Python's Future

- **AI and Data Science**: Python will remain the **dominant language** for **AI, machine learning**, and **data science**. Libraries like **TensorFlow, PyTorch, scikit-learn**, and

pandas are continuously improving, enabling more complex AI models, faster data processing, and more powerful analysis.

- **Web Development**: Frameworks like **Django** and **Flask** will continue to be widely used for **backend development**, especially for startups and rapid prototyping. Python's simplicity and readability make it a preferred choice for web developers.

- **Cloud Computing**: Python will remain a key player in cloud-native development, especially in platforms like **AWS Lambda** and **Azure Functions**, where Python is supported for **serverless computing**.

- **Automation**: Python will continue to be the go-to language for automating tasks, from server management to building CI/CD pipelines.

2. C#'s Future

- **Cross-Platform Development**: With the advent of **.NET Core** and **.NET MAUI, C#** will continue to thrive in the **cross-platform** development space. **.NET MAUI** (Multi-platform App UI) will allow developers to create **native mobile apps** for iOS, Android, macOS, and Windows with a single codebase.

- **Game Development**: **Unity**, powered by **C#**, will remain one of the most popular platforms for game development. As the **gaming industry** grows, C# developers will continue to be in demand for both mobile and console game development.

- **Cloud and Enterprise**: **C#** will remain a major language for building **enterprise applications** on **Azure**, particularly for industries that rely heavily on **.NET** technology stacks.

- **Microservices and Containers**: **C#** will continue to evolve in the microservices space, with developers leveraging **Docker** and **Kubernetes** for containerized applications. **ASP.NET Core** will be the backbone of many enterprise-grade, microservices-based systems.

3. Multi-Platform Development

- The future of **multi-platform development** is incredibly promising, with **Flutter, Xamarin, React Native**, and **.NET MAUI** leading the charge. These frameworks enable developers to build **cross-platform applications** (mobile, web, and desktop) using a single codebase.

- The rise of **Progressive Web Apps (PWAs)** will also allow developers to build web applications that work like native apps, offering greater flexibility for creating cross-platform experiences without the need for separate codebases for iOS, Android, and web platforms.

27.3 How to Stay Ahead and Continue Learning

To stay competitive in the ever-evolving world of software development, it's crucial to **embrace continuous learning**. Here are some ways you can ensure you remain at the forefront of the industry:

1. Keep Learning New Technologies

- **Explore New Frameworks**: Learn **Flutter, React Native, .NET MAUI**, and other emerging technologies for building cross-platform applications.
- **Deepen Your Knowledge in AI/ML**: As **AI** becomes more integrated into everyday software development, understanding **machine learning, deep learning**, and **data science** will be highly valuable.
- **Master Cloud Platforms**: Learn to work with **AWS, Azure**, or **Google Cloud Platform** to stay ahead in **cloud-native** development and **serverless computing**.

- **Experiment with Blockchain**: As blockchain continues to grow, learning about **smart contract development** and decentralized apps (dApps) will provide you with an edge in future tech landscapes.

2. Contribute to Open Source

Contributing to open-source projects helps you build a reputation in the community, collaborate with other developers, and learn new technologies. Open source allows you to experiment with **cutting-edge tools** and **frameworks**, expanding your knowledge base.

3. Build a Portfolio

Building a personal **portfolio** or **side projects** is a great way to showcase your skills. Whether it's a **SaaS product**, **mobile app**, or **AI model**, showcasing your work on platforms like **GitHub** can make you stand out to employers and clients.

4. Stay Updated with Industry Trends

- **Follow Blogs and Podcasts**: Subscribe to blogs, YouTube channels, and podcasts that discuss the latest trends in software development, AI, cloud computing, and mobile development.

- **Attend Conferences**: Participate in conferences, webinars, and meetups to stay updated on the latest trends and network with other professionals.
- **Join Developer Communities**: Engage with communities on **Stack Overflow, Reddit, Dev.to**, and **GitHub** to keep up with new tools, libraries, and industry developments.

5. Certifications and Online Courses

Certifications and courses can demonstrate your commitment to learning and advancing in your field. Look for certifications in:

- **Cloud Computing**: AWS, Azure, and Google Cloud certifications.
- **AI and Machine Learning**: TensorFlow, PyTorch, and Microsoft's AI certifications.
- **Mobile Development**: Xamarin, React Native, or Flutter certifications.

Platforms like **Coursera, Udemy, Pluralsight**, and **edX** offer high-quality courses on the latest technologies.

Conclusion

The future of software development is full of exciting opportunities, driven by advancements in **cloud computing, AI, mobile development,** and **cross-platform technologies**. To stay competitive, it's important to continuously expand your skillset, keep up with industry trends, and explore new technologies like **Python, C#,** and **multi-platform development**.

By **contributing to open-source projects, building a solid portfolio**, and embracing continuous learning, you can position yourself as a versatile developer ready to tackle the challenges of tomorrow's tech landscape.

Let's continue building and shaping the future of software development!